In the early hours of 31 August 1997, and beautiful woman, who just h famous woman in the world, died a car chase through the streets of paparazzi who so dominated her life.

How did this happen? How did a shy Sloane kindergarten teacher from the heart of England with no visible talents come to conquer the world in a manner which would make John F. Kennedy and Marilyn Monroe look like little more than home-town heroes? The answers are sought in this book, part love story, part document of our times.

Julie Burchill has written about and observed Diana with fascination for many years and first coined the phrase 'the People's Princess', which has become such a powerful shorthand slogan for all Diana stood for. Many books will be written about Diana, but the only precedent for this book will be Norman Mailer's *Marilyn*, reflecting both the author's love for her subject and the groundswell of popular anger against our ruling house that will invariably face the House of Windsor once the period of mourning is over. The Age Of Diana has not ended; rather, it is just beginning. Frozen forever at the height of her beauty and power by death, she will be the mourner at every royal wedding and the blushing bride at every Coronation. She will never be forgotten.

Julie Burchill has been a journalist from the age of seventeen. Since then she has worked for or contributed to most of the major newspapers and magazines on both sides of the Atlantic and in continental Europe. She has written novels and non-fiction which have been translated into a dozen languages; she has also written stage and television screenplays. In 1998 she published her autobiography *I Knew I Was Right*, as well as her latest novel. She was Editor-in-Chief of the magazine *The Modern Review* and is a columnist for the *Guardian*'s weekend section.

Diana

Julie Burchill

ORION

An Orion Paperback
First published in Great Britain by Weidenfeld & Nicolson in 1998
This paperback edition published in 1999 by
Orion Books Ltd,
Orion House, 5 Upper St Martin's Lane,
London WC2H 9EA

A CIP catalogue record for this book is
available from the British Library.

ISBN: 0 75282 589 5

Printed and bound in Great Britain by
Clays Ltd, St Ives plc

For Jack

contents

Foreword

UNFINISHED SYMPATHY

In the early hours of 31 August, 1997, a spirited, compassionate and beautiful Englishwoman – who just happened to be the most famous woman in the world – kept her final rendezvous with destiny in a tunnel under the asphalt of Paris, hunted down a hole like an animal by a pack of black leather pursuers riding screaming machines. She died in a German car with an Egyptian playboy in the French capital – irretrievably lost to the country which had raised her to be humane, witty and warm, and had loved her for these qualities; despite the fact that this country's ruling house had, in its turn, stalked, trapped, used and abused her before exiling her within her own country when her shining spirit and unprecedented popularity became too much for them. Who had, in fact, turned out to be the only people who could not love her.

How did this happen? How did a shy Sloane nursery teacher from the heart of England with no visible talents ('I'm thick as two short planks, me') come to conquer the world in a manner which would make the likes of John Kennedy and Marilyn Monroe seem little more than hometown heroes? How in the name of God, the God whom we call upon to save the Queen, did the House of Windsor imagine that the people would ever let them get away with their appalling treatment of such a rare, shining spirit? And how will we ever live without her?

The answer is, of course, that we won't. The Age Of Diana has not ended but has rather just begun. Frozen forever at the height of her beauty, compassion and power by death, she will be the mourner at every royal wedding and the blushing bride at every Coronation. We'll never forget her – and neither will they. The Queen is dead – long live the Queen.

Family

Affair

The strange and lonely childhood of Lady Diana Spencer;
the history of the vicious upper-class divorce

Chapter 1

Diana

Traditionally, in fairytales, the beautiful princess's birth is attended by a host of good fairies who contribute various presents of a character-building kind. But when Diana Spencer was born on the late afternoon of 1 July 1961, in Park House on the royal estate of Sandringham in Norfolk, it would be nice to think that the spirits of some of her extraordinarily wide range of distant relations, both living and dead, drew near to bestow their own gifts on this little girl.

Humphrey Bogart would have given her his toughness; Georges Sand her passion. Harriet Beecher Stowe would have given her her sympathy for the oppressed; Graham Greene his ability to seek out betrayal – and once established, not to despair but to somehow grow strong from the knowledge and the containment of it. Oliver Cromwell would have given her his contempt for the ruling house and Bismarck his taste for battle. Rudolf Valentino would have given her his weakness for the dramatic, and Orson Welles his gift for the framing of the perfect shot. Louisa May Alcott would have given her her idealism about the family, and Jane Austen her cynicism about marriage.

And Winston Churchill – Winston Spencer Churchill – would have made sure she understood that, once in a while, a public figure comes along who, though closely identified at first with the ruling house, goes on to mean much, much more to the people of that country than any cold, remote figurehead ever could. But of course, every christening has its Carabousse. And Diana Spencer's would have been her future step-grandmother, Barbara Cartland, who gave her a gift which was to irretrievably blight her short, sad, shimmering, spectacular life. The belief that there really was any such thing as a fairytale romance.

She should have known better, of course; as a child, right in front of her eyes, a fairytale romance which had enjoyed its day in the sun as the biggest society wedding of the year was coming apart with its last rites of rage and recrimination. From her ringside seat at the top of the stairs, the young Diana Spencer was given her first glimpses of marital combat and the chaos it can cause even in the most highly bred and established of households. The house of cards which has been built the highest will naturally make the biggest mess when it all falls down.

While it may be true, as Kierkegaard said, that life can only be lived forwards and understood backwards, the example of her parents' marriage might have given Diana some pause for thought before she embarked on her own conjugal climb. Frances Roche was eighteen years old that day in Westminster Abbey in 1954, when she swore obedience to the thirty-two-year-old Viscount Althorp, heir to the seventh Earl Spencer, watched by the Queen and her immediate family. Here it began: A Tale Of Two Families, irretrievably linked in love and hate as far as the eye, especially the eye of the ninth Earl Spencer, can see.

It does not take a particularly wild imagination to see marriage as a malignant minuet which historically has had far more to do with ownership and property than with love and affection. In cases where the modern companionate model has triumphed, the truth need not fear standing naked, and will probably prefer the good-humoured, clear-eyed straightforwardness of the registry office. But when there is a secret agenda rustling beneath the red carpet of romance, it is best that the disguises and decoys come thick and fast as confetti; the cathedrals huge enough for ghosts to watch unseen from the shadows, the choirs singing sweetly enough to drown out the reasons why these two people may not, must not be joined together, the cakes lush enough to feed the regiments who have died defending such privilege, the champagne filling more glasses than even the bride's tears will over the coming years. A wedding is a funeral which masquerades as a feast. And the greater the pageantry, the deeper the savagery.

When ordinary couples marry, there are obviously issues of property and ownership involved, but these may well begin and end with sexual continence and the company car. When the aristocracy marry, much more is involved. For instance, until some politician with more convictions than contortions comes forward and waves the piece of paper which abolishes that monumental blockage in the S-bend of public life we call the British monarchy, the only people who can affect their fortunes to the smallest degree are the aristocracy, who by a combination of treachery and marriage – often both served up in the same poisoned loving cup – have influenced and even toppled our ruling houses. To the Windsors, the aristocrats are commoners first and foremost – as Diana Spencer, the girl who was born a lady, made a royal and died stripped of her title, and as the People's Princess far more than the Windsors', would find out so hurtfully – but commoners who can actually touch them, and must therefore have a careful eye kept upon them. As the Queen with her husband, her sister and her mother were doing in Westminster Abbey that day in 1954, when the most beautiful debutante of her year reeled in the heir to a considerable fortune and a profoundly English history, full of snubbing, subversion, survivalism and self-made men.

Soon after the engagement of HRH Prince Charles and Lady Diana Spencer was announced, the Prince for some reason felt moved to announce proudly that his intended was 'far more English than me'. This might have been the first point the bumbling prince ever lost to the fast lady, apart, of course, from the famous, fatal 'Whatever love means. . .'. It wasn't exactly clever to rub the noses of the British people in the fact that their Royal Family was not only a dirty great con, but a dirty great foreign con, shipped in for reasons which had nothing to do with the good of this country and everything to do with the Shakespearean dramas ceaselessly being acted out in the drawing rooms of Europa. At Diana's wedding, with this thought firmly in mind, it was easy to see a beautiful Anglo-Saxon virgin captured and forcibly wed to a swarthy Graeco-German brigand prince among a great deal of pomp and circumstance hell bent on concealing a basic injustice; that perhaps the country belonged more to her people already – and by extension to all of us English commoners – than it did to the cold, remote Saxe-Coburg-Gothas, with their dry eyes and their supreme stage management.

Diana's father, the eighth Earl Spencer, who by this time had suffered a serious stroke and had never been too much of a swashbuckler anyway, looked somehow impeccably English – sentimental, obstinate, unpretentious – as he walked with his daughter down the aisle towards that other family, so replete in their health and wealth and hypocrisy and the well-hung, gamey, glittering medals they could never have earned, not in a million years. It had been this same Earl who, stroke or not, had had the wit to reply when questions were asked as to whether his daughter was good enough to marry a Windsor, whether indeed a Windsor was good enough to marry a Spencer.

He wasn't joking. At certain times over the past four centuries, the Spencers have been richer and more powerful than the ruling house. From their Tudor sheep-tending days they had reached the upper heights of the aristocracy by the reign of Charles II. The Spencers swished sure-footedly throughout England like Diana through Harvey Nichols at the height of her retail therapy craze. They married the Churchills, the Dukes of Marlborough, adding the dynasty's power and money to their endless rollover; as the historian John Pearson put it, 'There seemed no stopping the Spencers as they swept up heiresses and estates, bought great libraries and paintings at knock-down prices and built London's most ravishing Palladian mansions to house them. By the zenith of the eighteenth century, almost everyone who was anyone in politics and society seemed to be related to the Spencers who were at the centre of what someone called "the great Whig cousinage".' We don't think much of the Whigs today, but at the time they passed for decent in the cesspool of English politics – actually, the Whigs make New Labour look positively and rabidly right-wing. In the nineteenth century, the Spencer politicians backed adult suffrage and Irish reform; their surliness seemed bred in the bone, from the time when Sir John Spencer, the richest of all the Elizabethan sheep-masters, was the first to do business direct with London. His son bought himself a title from the broke James I, but the Spencers gave a wide berth to the corrupt and clueless court while the next Spencer heir, William, refused the royal offer of an earldom for ten thousand pounds.

The Spencers spurned the crown once it had outlived its original usefulness, and relied on sheep, land and marriage for money; very much the working-class way. From the word go, the Spencers married out whenever there was a choice between blue blood and being in the black, even though they were already rich; they married Kitson girls and Poyntz girls, the dowry-heavy daughters of City tycoons. It may be bold to venture the idea that a lady whose surname ends in one of the last three letters of the alphabet is of Jewish extraction, but venture it I would. From the moment I first saw her, Diana Spencer seemed in some small way Jewish to me – profoundly maternal, disliking horses, strong-nosed, comely, needing too much and giving too much – and I cannot think of any identifying marks on an incoming bride more likely to annoy the deeply Anglo-Saxon and outdoorsy Royal Family than these.

And so the first of the second line of Spencer aristocrats, his title of Earl given free of charge by William Pitt who was in need of Spencer's support, married Georgiana Poyntz, rich, beautiful and intelligent. Their heir was born to schedule. But their daughters were the deadly weapons, as Spencer girls would be. The then Prince of Wales fell in love with Harriet, the elder Spencer sister. She felt nothing for him and made this clear in spades, marrying the dishy Earl of Bessborough instead. Much later, Prince Charles would have to stomach his girlfriend Sarah Spencer telling *Woman's Own*, of all the lowbrow forums, that her feelings for her alleged boyfriend were the same as they might be for the big brother she had never had and that the relationship was, therefore, platonic.

Georgiana soon found that revenge was a dish best eaten with two spoons and took several lovers to lighten her darkness

Harriet's sister Georgiana, like Sarah's sister Diana, was not so lucky. When she was seventeen, she made a match that blighted her life, a marriage to the older Duke of Devonshire. The Duke, par for the course, was not in love with her but with his long-term mistress, and had seen their union as a merger rather than a marriage – he asked for her hand, but wanted her land. In love with her husband but by no means stupid, Georgiana soon found that revenge was a dish best eaten with two spoons and took several lovers to lighten her darkness.

But the shooting-star quick-fix of sex proved insufficient for Georgiana, and she began to use her beauty, charm and position to publicize the causes she believed in. In 1774 she campaigned for her Whig friend Charles James Fox by giving kisses to the butchers of Long Acre in return for votes. Centuries later, Diana would give kisses to the butchers of Fleet Street in return for their votes.

The eighteenth-century Spencers were prancing, leaping gazelles, stylish and supple; the nineteenth-century Spencers were idealistic and evangelistic. Often acting against the interests of their class by following their consciences, they helped secure the passage of the Reform Act of 1832, and in the case of the fifth Earl, John Poyntz Spencer – the Red Earl – gave Wimbledon Common to the people. But by the twentieth century, the Spencers were in retreat, away from the hurly-burly of public life and into the cloistered world of the professional courtier class. The sixth Earl Spencer was a man with few interests beyond pomp, pageantry and uniforms, and was rewarded for abandoning his Whig heritage by being appointed Groom-in-Waiting to Queen Victoria. The seventh Earl, a withdrawn man made bitter by the dramatic decline of the Spencers as a force to be reckoned with, withdrew into the private splendours of Althorp House, where he would sit for hours with Queen Mary in the Great Hall, both of them engrossed in their embroidery.

His son, Diana's father, was unrecognizable as one of that glittering Whig cousinage; he was a catalogue of complaints — against his father whom he hated, against Althorp 'the

11

Diana

Mausoleum', against university which he had neither use nor ability for – trapped in a vacuum. After joining the Guards, he was appointed equerry to the Queen, a largely ceremonial situation which suited his limited pockets of talent perfectly. The Spencers, then, had come full circle as they battened down the hatches, unable and unwilling to meet the challenges of social change. In the space of five hundred years they had gone from being stubborn, self-reliant men who refused offers of titles from the crown to being sleepwalking servants of a monarchy also in decline.

The aristocracy gossip over garden fences like any other set of people forced together by circumstances of birth. Those fences may well separate hundreds of thousands of acres rather than scrubby back yards, and that land may house hundreds of workers rather than a couple of gnomes. But what is perhaps most unforgivable about the English ruling class – apart from their stupidity, ignorance and casual cruelty – is their stinginess. They will plot and intrigue and connive to hold onto their ten-thousandth acre as if it was their first and last.

This is where the mutual need of the aristocracy and the monarchy is at its starkest and bleakest. The aristocratic families wish to hold what they have, and if possible add to it; the example of many once-great houses, which have disappeared as surely as the Shulamites and the Moabites from the Bible, puts urgency into their usually slothful limbs. The monarchy never has any trouble holding onto what it has; but on the other hand, its genes aren't in the best of states in which to husband it. It remains a bitter paradox of monarchy that it is based on a hereditary principle which leaves those very heirs incapable of living up to their exalted roles due to the terrible state of a gene pool kept gasping for oxygen by the narrowness of the net cast when it comes to breeding. Hence the very striking picture-book 'princeliness' of William, son of a prince and a commoner, as opposed to the rather tragic and malformed aspect of Charles, Heir Apparent, the son of a prince and a princess. The bad blood of a billion Battenburgs, Hanovers and Saxe-Coburg-Gothas fetched up in the young generation of the House of Windsor; new blood was needed. And this time, the Windsors would not have far to look.

Ruth Gill was a young Scotswoman who had had the good luck and judgement to marry a rich Irish-American who, as people do, inherited the all but useless Irish title of fifth Baron Fermoy. A charming and canny couple, they became close to the then Duke and Duchess of York – better known now as the Queen Mother and that poor man she married. Their friendship flourished after the abdication made the Yorks King and Queen, and the Fermoys went to live on the Sandringham estate. The Sandringham estate now sounds eerily like a run-down inner-city sin-bin somewhere in the West Midlands, where the law of the jungle rules and every family lives in fear of that family; the one so mean and dumb and sprawling, the one that just doesn't care.

Ruth Fermoy became a Woman of the Bedchamber to her friend, an unwholesomely rompish title which does indeed conjure up images of the two women, the Queen and her

13

courtier, sitting up late into the night toasting marshmallows, sipping Horlicks and nipping gin and deciding just which unfortunate girl's life they were going to blight next with their coy and callous nudges towards death by premature matrimony. The first up for the honour was Lady Fermoy's own daughter Frances Roche, whose high spirits and sexiness must have invariably come across as nothing but trouble to these two prim, marriage-made Scotswomen. And poor old Johnnie Spencer, bless him, never too bright, just rattling around Court, up to inherit that lovely house one day. . .There must have been more than a little Beefeater spilled in excitement on the Bedchamber floor the night they cooked that one up.

Hatched, matched and dispatched; now the couple would work towards the heir and the spare

And so the eighteen-year-old Frances was set up with the thirty-two-year-old Johnnie and the biggest society wedding of the year took place under the watchful eye of the House of Windsor. Hatched, matched and dispatched; now the couple would work towards the heir and the spare. All the ingredients for a solid, smug upper-class marriage seemed set in place, as they had already been set in stone throughout the ages.

But something happened. The Honourable Frances Roche now had the Spencer name and she began to behave like one. Her high style and headstrong nature, even in her teens, recalled the Spencer girls of the eighteenth century; her immediate plunge into pregnancy and childbirth as a full-time job cannot have sat easily with these qualities. And the glitches began. She obediently gave birth nine months after her wedding, but it was to a girl, Sarah, and then another girl, Jane. The heir, John, was born in 1960 but died within ten hours. When Diana was born on 1 July 1961, her parents were so sure she was a boy that no female name had even been considered. Finally the fifth child, Charles Althorp himself, was born in 1964, and only then, with four children under the age of ten, was Frances allowed to stop breeding. She was only twenty-eight.

Upper-class women of her day did not generally expect marriage to be one long romantic game of kiss-chase, but the manner in which she had been used as a machine to incubate an heir for a much older man, as upper-class women regularly are, cannot have pleased a woman as young and spirited as Frances. Housed in the Fermoys' former home on the estate at Sandringham, she must have thought at times that her life was over. Her mother must have imagined her plan had worked. But there was something wrong with this picture, something wrong which would give Frances' life back to her again. It was the swinging sixties; just down the road from sleepy Norfolk, slowly but surely coming up towards the gates of the Royal

Diana

Estate. The sixties would bring her freedom and a second marriage to a man who was nothing more arcane and aristocratic than the heir to a wallpaper fortune. It was 1967, the summer of love. Frances must have felt great when she ran away with him that November. Her mother must have had a fit.

'Rich bitch'; a ringing, resonant, easily accessed oath. Far more so than 'rich bastard', the cursing of rich women has become an increasingly popular soft option as actual political analysis and action have decreased. Men who consider foxhunting a matter of personal choice, for instance, will happily subscribe to the notion that IT TAKES NINE DUMB ANIMALS TO MAKE A FUR COAT BUT ONLY ONE DUMB ANIMAL TO WEAR IT.

Such selective class-hatred may well soothe the soreness of the spare squalid male. But it remains a fact that upper-class women are, when the chips are down and the divorce is being drawn up, women first and foremost, and are privileged and protected only so far as they agree to be treated as property; production lines wearing pearls. An upper-class woman who fails to honour the contract, whatever the conduct of her husband, cannot expect her class position to protect her from a legal attack far more sustained and vicious than most which take place between divorcing couples with less to lose. The chivalry on which upper-class men like to pride themselves evaporates immediately in the face of female refusal, and the dissenting aristocratic woman can expect a merciless public attack on her reputation of a type that a gangland murderer would be very wary of inflicting upon his moll.

The sad and strange case of Margaret, Duchess of Argyll is an example of just how vicious the aristocracy can get. In 1960 she was taken to court by her ex-secretary Yvonne MacPherson, charged with libel and slander. The charges seemed rather pallid for such purple words; the Duke had left his wife and gone to live at Claridges, and when Margaret asked newspapermen where they had obtained their information, they named Miss MacPherson. The Duchess' subsequent accusation to MacPherson's face was the cause of the court case – piquantly, Margaret was performing in a beauty pageant as Marie Antoinette when the court papers were served on her, wearing a borrowed necklace which had once actually belonged to the French queen who serves to this day as the archetypal rich bitch Aunt Sally for the excesses originating with her husband and his ruling house.

Starting small, the case quickly gathered steam and became a public scandal – although the real scandal was the way the woman involved was treated. Margaret's husband Ian, the eleventh Duke of Argyll, referred to her throughout as 'Satan'; his defence counsel, Gilbert Beyfus, called her 'a poisonous liar'. The Duke was a violent and heavy drinker in the habit of greeting each fruitful new dawn with a glass of neat gin, yet the Duchess was completely and unequivocally painted as the villain of both the piece and the marriage. She was accused of insanity by her husband, who went on to prove his stability by showing up at a lunch in America she was attending, saying that he had something amusing to show the party. These turned out to be a packet of pornographic pictures; the man and the woman were unrecognizable as the snapper had conveniently cut his subjects' heads off, but the woman – the fellatrix, kneeling in front of a naked man – was wearing pearls similar to a type owned by the Duchess.

Appalled, she returned to London in order to divorce him. When the libel case came to court, Margaret was advised not to take the stand; she was already an upper-class woman relieved of her protection and thus under marching orders to some-where beyond the Pale – although she ended up as a gay icon, somewhere over the rainbow. She lost the case, was landed with the heavy costs (appropriately, as the Duke of Argyll had always told his friends that he only married the independently wealthy Margaret in order to get his bills paid) and then went straight into her divorce.

The Duke was a violent, amphetamine-addicted drunkard who had cut short his honeymoon in order to get back to his London clubs. In the first four weeks of their blessed union, the Argylls had two writs for unpaid bills served upon them which Margaret's father settled (one from Worth for a mink coat that the Duke had fancied for his previous wife) even after he had given Argyll a quarter of a million pounds on his marriage to Margaret to help pay the death duties on Inveraray Castle, the family seat. When the Duke sought divorce in 1963 on the grounds of adultery, you would hardly have believed he could be called an inno-cent party. Yet in his summing up Judge Lord Wheatley was merciless;

The photographs. . .not only establish that the defender was carrying on an adulterous association with those other men or man but that the defender was a highly sexed woman who had ceased to be satisfied with normal relations and had started to indulge in what I can only describe as disgusting sexual activities in order to gratify a basic sexual appetite. (*The Times*, 9 May 1963)

Remember, this was not the England of the prime-time cathode confessional and lap-dancing, but of white gloves and the *Light Programme*. Such a report in *The Times* was tantamount to slapping a scarlet letter 'A' on a woman's back and forcing her to wear it in front of her friends and family in the Royal Enclosure at Ascot. Margaret of Argyll learned the hard way that upperclass women are women first and foremost, and that their class privilege counts for less than zero if they in any way rebel against the men they marry. Margaret was used as an example to other women of her class who might have had an eye for a pretty boy or the stomach for a fight. She was used as a svelte, couture-clad scarecrow left standing there, stark and shocked and skeletal, to warn other well-heeled women passing by that you could come from money and go to Heathfield and be presented at Court and fourteen years after your marriage at the Brompton Oratory you could have your dress copied by Norman Hartnell for the wedding of Princess Elizabeth, but if you wanted your freedom, it would still count for less than zero.

going over the top and running for their lives with wallpaper heirs and polo players

Yet still they came; the stubborn Shires girls, childhood sweethearts who wanted to grow up, 'old girls' who wanted to be young women, mothers who wanted to be lovers – all of them wearing nursery food like badges of honour on their twinsets, going over the top and running for their lives with wallpaper heirs and polo players. These were the women whose conjugal situations had become so unbearable that they would leave their own children rather than continue with the living death of a used-up marriage. They were the walking wounded who suddenly found their running shoes.

After many years of acrimony, Frances Spencer left in 1967, a year heavy with associations of permissiveness, self-expression and the winds of social and sexual change whistling through the phoney peace of the post-War English counties, starting her divorce proceedings the following year on the grounds of her husband's cruelty. Earl Spencer counter-claimed on grounds of adultery. After much expenditure and publicity, Frances was forced to drop her case – the fate of Margaret of Argyll never far from her mind – and the Earl was granted a divorce against her. Then the real fight started and the real damage was done.

Although she filed for custody of her four children, although her children had been, and had taken up, her whole life since she was nineteen and although it was normal for custody to be awarded to the mother, the slippery deck was stacked against Frances from the start; snobbery and misogyny saw to that, and a woman who deserted an earl must have seemed, in the context of pre-Swinging Britain, not only immoral but mad. But the cream of the joke and the nail in the coffin came when her mother, Lady Fermoy, emerged from lurking in the Queen Mother's bedchamber just long enough to put the boot in on the side of the Earl.

It is not too much of an imaginative feat to feel that the old lady's main motivation was not the mental health of her grandchildren – who would almost certainly have been happier with their mother – but rather equal parts pique and panic. Pique that the daughter she had so single-mindedly set up (as one would the victim of a confidence trick, perhaps) in so stellar a marriage had seen fit to fly the coop; and panic that her grandchildren, her only remaining hostages to the future, might now grow up not as the girls-next-door to the Windsors, but rather as sunburned little Aussies with wide open voices and a background in trade. Surely anything, even tearing them from their mother's arms, seemed preferable to such a *déclassé* fate for a family to whom being courtiers had become the only possible life choice.

Card games were popular among the young Spencers on

Diana

those long echoing evenings in Park House on the Sandringham estate under the watchful eye of the House of Windsor, as the sixties swung to a close, but I would bet that Happy Families was not one of them. There is something almost uncomprehensibly sad about the separation of a mother from her child, recalling as it does the initial separation which pushes the child into a harsh and frightening world, and that this almost metaphysically melancholy loneliness can have been deliberately engineered by the father of that child – as it is when a man gains custody – and even by the mother's mother in the name of nothing more than dynastic power and the hereditary principle, is as damning an indictment of the heart-lessness of the English ruling class as it is possible to imagine.

Ironically, it is the upper-class woman who is most likely to lose her children, and the upper-class woman who has been brought up to be nothing but a wife and mother. When they are parted from each other and when that separation is compounded by the additional separation of boarding school, surely all the signals are set in place for an adulthood fraught with insecurity, loneliness and a strange feeling of being in exile, almost. In Mrs Shand Kydd, in her search for religious solace and her solitary travels, and then in her daughter Diana, alone at Christmas in her apartments at Kensington Palace while her boys unwrapped presents from their loving Granny in cold, hard Balmoral, we saw the ultimate heartbreaking result of one family's destructive desire to be, first and foremost, a vessel of the ruling house.

Royalty has never been elected; it derives its power solely from the hereditary principle. This principle gives constitutional weight and importance to the apparently most private of actions; conception, birth, marriage, adultery, death. This is reflected in the fact that well into this century a member of the government had to be present at the birth of royal children. This is why adultery with the wife of the monarch is a treasonable offence. This could well be why, on the announcement of her betrothal, Diana's uncle felt it appropriate to confirm to the world that she was indeed a virgin, and why Diana herself once said that throughout her teenage years she never indulged in the usual pleasures of the flesh 'because I knew I had to keep myself tidy for what lay ahead'. This is why a ruling house has no right to expect privacy.

But what a sad, soul-destroying life this is. To be born into such a sorrowful state can be dismissed as an accident; to engineer entry into such an existence, ostensibly on behalf of someone under one's care and protection, seems an act of unqualified cruelty. But marrying her daughter into the Spencer family was, it turned out, merely the dress rehearsal. Lady Fermoy's greatest plan was just a twinkle in her grandmotherly eye as she watched the little girl Diana, whom she had made motherless, play.

Uptown

Girl

The making of a super Sloane

Chapter 2

the upper-class woman to this day receives an education fit only for a child or a cretin

It is an accepted wisdom that the upper and working classes have a good deal in common while men and women in the middle classes are different. For a long time, one of the most striking examples of this was the way the working and upper classes failed to educate their daughters, while the middle classes assumed that girls were as likely to benefit from an education as boys. In fact, in recent years it actually seems from exam results that education might actually be more suitable for girls than for boys, who increasingly seem to see it as an imposition which keeps them away from the football pitch and the Nintendo screen.

Until quite recently, working- and upper-class girls were educated for little more than marriage, motherhood and housekeeping. This changed for most of the population when women entered the job market, and now the average working-class girl's education is indistinguishable from that of her brother as it is assumed she will need to work for her living as much as he will. For the upper-class girl, this revolution never happened; necessity not coming into the equation, they were never allowed to invent themselves.

Instead the upper-class woman to this day receives an education fit only for a child or a cretin, centred completely around the happy home she is fated to create one day. Upper-class women are kept ignorant because it is presumed that uneducated women will be less likely to strop or stray than their bluestockinged sisters. But on the contrary, it would appear that when a woman's mind has no capacity to amuse or entertain her during separation from her husband, her body will step in smartish and go to bed early with a good looker as opposed to a good book. Worse, in the absence of intellectual interests, jerry-built 'spiritual' ones will come to the fore, as they do in unschooled pockets of the female working class, and we will be treated to such unedifying spectacles as the younger generation of royal princesses and duchesses having their rectums flushed out with gallons of soapy water, sitting smugly under plastic pyramids and being held in the thrall of clairvoyants. The crueller ones simply go out and torture animals when they are bored. Surely having your daughter taught the finer points of appreciating George Eliot's *Middlemarch* would be preferable, cheaper and far less embarrassing in the long run.

But at many of the leading girls' schools in this country, upper-class parents habitually shell out large sums of money in order that their daughters are instructed in such vital issues as how to make beds, embroider, arrange flowers and cook. After ten years of this, they take jobs which will exercise these talents to the full. They become caterers and florists if they are really straining at the leash to be career girls. But this is

Diana

generally thought to be a bit extreme, and the women who pursue such lives in the fast lane are probably NQOT (not quite our type) – probably some foreign blood in there somewhere.

No, normally, in a Marie Antoinette-playing-at-milkmaids sort of way, they will play at being junior housewives, bringing up other people's babies and soufflés in equal parts. But there cannot help but be an element of unreality about their lives which gives it a hollow, slightly sad feel. Lady Diana Spencer cuddled and cleaned for a living, but lived in an extremely expensive flat in SW London. Upper-class girls do domestic, low-paid work not because they have to economically, but because they feel they are not fit for anything else. And after ten years of being turned into flower-arranging, soufflé-cooking zombies, they often aren't. The irony is that the only thing they are trained for – domesticity – will often be handed over to the attention of paid employees when they marry. A woman who has been trained only to cook and look after children will feel utterly useless and bereft when her children go to boarding school and her husband is forever eating at his club.

Brasher, flashier girls might find work in art galleries or publishing, as did Sarah Ferguson, or even as It Girls, simply showing off. It was typical of Lady Diana Spencer's insecurity, kindness and low expectations that even though she came from one of England's oldest families she opted for none of these. At school she had been known as 'Thicky' Spencer, and it was her lack of success during her schooldays, as surely as being deprived of her mother at the age of six, which gave her that lack of edge, that excess of humility and humanity, which made the British people from the word go ignore her title and see her as 'one of us'. We could tell she'd already been hurt; that was why she was one of us. Because she already knew how hard life was.

It was hardly the School Of Hard Knocks where she had learned this; more the School Of Long Separations. It remains one of the mysteries of the aristocracy exactly why they feel the need to send their children to boarding school and why at such an early age; certain schools will accept children as full-time boarders from the age of six, which never fails to amaze foreigners. For a class that cleaves to continuity as fiercely as it does, there is a tremendous amount of putting asunder within it and by the time he or she is sixteen, the young upper-class boy or girl must feel as though there is already something amoeba-like about their young lives – forever dividing and separating and subdividing, and always the fear in the back of the mind that one has left an important part of oneself some-where along the way, never to be recovered.

As early as January 1968, when Diana Spencer was starting at Silfield day school in King's Lynn, recovery was already on her mind. Her mother gone, her father bitter and brooding, her immediate interest and talent even as a six-year-old lay in helping out with those even younger than her in the nursery class. Throughout her life, Diana seemed instinctively to understand that the only way she could harness and heal her own pervading sorrow was to help others; by reaching out to

29

Diana

touch, she too would be comforted. In later years she became the only member of the Royal Family not to wear gloves when meeting the public; the laying on of hands had to be carried out to the letter or else she might falter and fall.

At the age of nine she was sent to Riddlesworth Hall boarding school at Diss in Norfolk. Her homesickness has been well documented, but it does behove us to spend a moment's silence imagining exactly why a nine-year-old girl, who is in the process of being trained for nothing more strenuous than running a large house, needed to be sent away from home full time at such a young age. She was not being trained for the armed forces or for the stage; there was no need for her to learn team spirit, because she would never have to work in a team. One comes to the unwholesome and sad conclusion that boarding school is – like being 'blooded' with the blood of the hunted fox while not yet in their teens – just another of the grim and self-loathing ways this brutish class 'toughens up' its young as preparation for a life in which sensitivity, beauty and empathy will be conspicuous by their absence. Yet again, you have to wonder if making life better might not be preferable to making people worse.

Diana spent much of her time with Peanuts, her guinea pig, who lived in the school's Pets' Corner with a selection of mice, hamsters and rabbits belonging to other pupils; here the young girl could pad quietly at night when in need of the affection or intellectual stimulation that such schools notoriously fail to provide. Over the next three years she would see far more of Peanuts than of her parents, who visited her on alternate weekends bringing Twiglets, Creme Eggs and ginger biscuits. She was already becoming the persona we think of today, a lithe and shiny mermaid only at home and safe from harm – if not from prying eyes – when playing in the water with her sons, and swimming was her greatest school achievement. Even though she was to die on land – worse, underground; as though she was, ever-helpful, getting into her grave prematurely – Diana's life recalls many images of drowning. There is Lichtenstein's *Girl Drowning*, in which the tragic beauty dies rather than ask the lover who has hurt her for help, and of course Stevie Smith's poem *Not Waving But Drowning*. From the first time she waved to us from that glass coach, leaving the wedding she had approached 'like a lamb to the slaughter', she was signalling for help.

Diana could have ridden horses at Riddlesworth Hall but – in her first open rebellion against the rituals of her class – she chose to dance, taking extra lessons in ballet which she had been learning since the age of three. She was 'obsessed', 'mad keen' about dancing, and had 'always' wanted to be a ballerina. Ballet is the strangest of all art forms, the most escapist and yet the most demanding; requiring from its audience an utter enchantment which if given freely can transport them. Both performer and audience must enter into a complicity of belief in the power of beauty; if they can suspend their cumbersome common sense for long enough, they will enter another world. The unreality of *pointe* dancing, the gravity-defying leaps and the outlandish garb combine with the themes of tragedy, betrayal and madness to create a strange,

Diana

surreal spectacle particularly appealing to young women
afflicted by a non-specific sorrow which they do not have the
words to express – or which they do, but do not want to speak
aloud for fear of ridicule.

In the Broadway musical *A Chorus Line*, a song called 'At
The Ballet' juxtaposes the troubled and insecure life of a young
girl, her parents locked in marital combat, with the sensations
of release and rapture she experiences at the ballet;
'Everything was beautiful at the ballet'. In later years, Diana's
favourite ballets – *Giselle*, *Sleeping Beauty* and particularly
Swan Lake – would seem almost tragically apt, with their
deceived and bewitched and grief-stricken heroines driven to
the brink of madness or the arms of Morpheus by the wiles of
witches and the perfidy of princes.

Her ambition as a young girl was to be a professional
dancer; a poignant twist on the usual routine of the showgirl
who dreams of being a princess. But she grew too tall; 'I over-
shot the height by a long way. I couldn't imagine some man
trying to lift me up'. Diana's tallness was an essential part of
her; a short Diana is not easily imagined. It was the immediate
thing that marked her out from the stunted Windsors, long
before all the other stuff started; it marked her out as a shining
star, a blonde beacon, easily seen by the crowds who would
visibly groan when she took the other side of the street during
walkabouts and they were stuck with him. Her tallness was a
barometer of her belief in herself; at first, in love, on show, she
was forever stooping, standing on lower steps, slouching
about in flat heels. Then, as her heart was broken and her fate

was sealed and her star was ascending into the stratosphere, she began to wear towering heels, big hats, baseball caps and upswept hair, taking her five foot ten-and-a-half inches up past the six foot mark which, in a blonde, denotes a flashy trophy armpiece of the sort beloved of short, dark, lecherous men. It was only when she stopped being a rich man's plaything that she allowed herself the ironic luxury of looking like one.

Diana left Riddlesworth Hall with only a prize for helpfulness to show for her years there. Her headmistress recalled her as 'decent and kind. . .everyone seemed to like her. What stands out in my mind is how awfully sweet she was with the little ones'. In September of 1973, she arrived at West Heath, a girls' boarding school in Kent where her sisters Jane and Sarah had divided the prizes between them; she swam and danced as if her life depended on it and treated her lessons as though her life was already over, failing to pick up even one O Level and spending her prep time reading Barbara Cartland novels by the score. At night she slept in a bed directly beneath a portrait of the Prince of Wales at his investiture; the Feng Shui of this set-up seems regrettable in retrospect. As Barbara Cartland herself proclaimed after the royal wedding: 'Just like a Barbara Cartland novel, dashing and adored, the Prince of Wales fell in love with the sweet, gentle, shy little girl who loved children.' As in the *wayang*, the shadow puppet plays of Indonesia, everything seemed to be slipping seamlessly into place, setting the little girl up for her fate even as she slept.

In 1975 the seventh Earl Spencer died and Diana lost her home at Park House at Sandringham when her father

Diana

inherited Althorp, home of fifteen generations of Spencers from 1508. It was not a happy house; and the house which had witnessed the Spencers' dramatic fall from being forceful and stylish mavericks to mere courtiers to the Crown cannot have been the happiest backdrop to the Earl's later life, his wife long gone, the children he had taken from their mother scattered at schools across the wistfully named Home Counties. Like Diana, he sought refuge in a Barbara Cartland creation; her daughter, Raine, whom he married in 1976. 'Raine saved my life', he said, after she nursed him through the stroke and coma which, two years later, seemed like the final sly blow to the robust glamour of the Spencers.

It was 1977 and the *wayang* was working out nicely now, as well as even Lady Fermoy could have hoped. Like a game of Patience played by some great spiteful hand, the elements were being put in place which would help to make Diana such fair game, such easy prey. Her beloved father brought home a woman his children detested on sight, further alienating Diana from what passed as her home, Althorp. Her mind by now rendered a barren Cartlandian mulch, combined with her insecurity and dreaminess, saw to it that she failed every single O Level she sat – in English Language, English Literature, Geography and Art – in the summer of 1977 and then again in the winter when she tried again before leaving at Christmas. She was given a special award brought out occasionally for pupils whose efforts had 'gone unsung' (rather as the Academy suddenly finds a Lifetime Achievement Award for a film star they have always considered too *déclassé* to reward, just as he is about to die) for services to the school, and told the headmistress that this was 'one of the most surprising things' that had ever happened to her. The familiar adult pattern of failure, persistence and low self-esteem was hers before she was old enough to vote – her world and her dominion before she had ever left the country or worn a crown.

Her beloved father brought home a woman his children detested on sight

It was in this weakened state that she renewed her acquaintance with Prince Charles, who had first cast eyes upon her when he was sixteen and she was a three-year-old neighbour, sitting on the floor of her nursery at Park House when he put his head around the door – if their positions could have remained like this, no doubt the marriage might have been happier, for the Windsors at least. She had, over the years, got to know the younger Princes Andrew and Edward, who, when staying at Sandringham, would come over to use Earl Spencer's swimming pool. But the chance of conversing with the Prince of Wales in all his Olympian glory was surely a treat worth waiting for.

Diana

'The ploughed field' close to 'Norbottle Wood' where Diana met Charles during the shoot at Althorp has attained the status of the famous Dallas 'grassy knoll' in the annals of modern royalty, and fittingly, because this is where the hunter got the game in the sights. Though who was hunter and who was hunted at this point is questionable. Virginal as she was, with a head full of fairytales, it is more than likely that Diana developed a massive crush on the Prince very quickly, though marriage could have hardly been on her mind; her sister Sarah, whom she idolized, was his girlfriend. Even later, when she naively believed that she was stalking him, her strings were being pulled. The sad fact is that both of these ill-matched people were game, fair prey to the dynastic ambitions of her family and the desire to strengthen the line of succession which troubled his. The difference is that he was old enough to know better.

Upon their engagement in 1981, Diana Spencer and Charles Windsor submitted to a five-minute-long television interview which was witnessed by 500 million people around the world. What did she think of him when she met him that day in the ploughed field near Norbottle Wood? 'Pretty amazing.' What did he think of her? 'I remember thinking what a very jolly and amusing and attractive sixteen-year-old she was. I mean, great fun – bouncy and full of life and everything.'

Examining the utterances of the Prince of Wales, it is a constant amazement that Joseph Conrad managed to write so well in his second language when the Heir Apparent of our own country has such an unfortunate way with his first. What a way to talk of one's first impression of the betrothed one is about to marry in front of millions of people! It's that 'and everything' that does it – not as cringingly awful as 'whatever love is', but close. It remains one of the puzzles of our age that one of the people who cannot speak what is widely known as the Queen's English would appear to be her son and heir.

So what would he have thought of the sixteen-year-old Diana Spencer? To give him credit, he would not have thought of her lecherously. The Prince of Wales has never been a pram-chaser, and has from his first girlfriend, Lucia Santa Cruz, valued experience rather than virtue in his female friends. When Barbara Cartland claimed that the pair were characters – or rather, cyphers – straight out of one of her books, she missed the important point that in real life the dashing hero would never, if left to his own devices, have pursued the fawn-like ingenue but would instead have been willingly vamped by a female of the feline, foxy or equine persuasion; one of those user-friendly, unmarriageable divorcees or widows whom Miss Cartland has so memorably pronounced that men may 'practise' their sexual skills on rather than deflower the true object of their affection.

While expecting complete compliance from his girlfriends, you got the impression that he wanted this compliance glossed with a hard shell of feistiness; that, ever the horseman, he wanted something worth breaking in, something that would give him a bit of a fight – John Wayne telling a Saracen princess that she was beautiful when angry before putting her over his knee. He often got the balance wrong, of course, and his dithering ways tipped many of the women he was fondest of – Camilla Shand, Jane Wellesley, Anna 'Whiplash' Wallace – over into showing the full extent of their feistiness by dropping him. As his father, with typical tact and tastefulness, was forever reminding him, 'If you don't get married soon, there won't be any girls left.'

So when he looked at the chubby, healthy sixteen-year-old, who had by this time developed a hearty, Sloaney breeziness to cover up her deep feelings of being 'very detached from everybody else. . .very different from everyone else', as she told Andrew Morton, he probably saw what everyone else saw: Sarah's younger sister, 'Thicky' Spencer, not an O Level to her name, who at this time seemed to derive her greatest satisfaction in life from waiting hand and foot on her clever, red-haired, difficult sister when she was at home for weekends with her smart London friends. Among them, of course, was the Prince of Wales.

Diana must have seemed utterly, boringly compliant and therefore uninteresting to him then. Later, of course, things would change; he would take home a Dresden shepherdess and arouse in her a Dresden bomber. And by the time, secure as the mother of the princes, she was confident enough to show her true Spencer nature, he was horrified. Diana never got the balance right when it came to attracting him; she was too good for that, too much her own person and, as his wife rather than his mistress, she didn't need to.

Diana was never a 'fascinating' mixture of the docile and the dangerous, as powerless upper-class women have been taught to be from Day One in order to snare a husband; she was true, either one thing or the other, a person who was actually growing and changing in a world where growing and changing is considered desirable only for gardens. Her personality was never something she put in the shop window in order to lure passersby; from the beginning, you feel she was a mystery and a sorrow to herself, then tentatively a challenge, and towards the end a triumph and a joy. She was never a plaything; she was always a work in progress.

Still, there was much work to be done on a sixteen-year-old girl with nothing to show for her needlessly expensive education but a headful of dreams, and in the best tradition of the English upper classes, good money was thrown after bad – when Diana was sent to a 'finishing school', the Institut Alpin Videmanette in Switzerland. The double meaning of the word 'finish' is irresistible; in theory, the girls were being 'finished' by being given a gloss, a final high polishing before they entered the marriage market. In practice it was the final insult against a group of young women who had frittered away their schooldays being instructed in fripperies which gave them next to no value in the jobs market or on the career ladder; now, just to rub it in, they would be instructed in the finer points of skiing, dressmaking and cordon bleu cookery. And if they weren't essentially finished off once and for all by this, they never would be.

Diana

Diana rebelled. Horribly homesick, she refused to speak the mandatory French and spent many sad hours planning her escape and writing home the letters she hoped would free her; the Prisoner of Wales, as one day she would mockingly call herself, was already learning the furtive habits of the ambitious captive. After a couple of months she hit on the ruse of reminding her father how expensive her school was, considering that she was getting nothing from it. The old rich are the old rich because, unlike the new rich, they don't waste money. Within weeks she was going home, where the heartbreak was.

Not that she wanted to go home as such; not where Acid Raine ruled as chatelaine. 'I was itching to go to London', Diana told Andrew Morton, when speaking of her frustration at not yet being eighteen, the magic age at which her parents agreed she could move to the capital.

The landed upper classes have always had a love-hate relationship with London, especially when it comes to their daughters being there unchaperoned. The squares may be pretty, and better still, named after one's ancestors, but really. . . In the mid-eighties, I knew of a situation in which three separate upper-class families in one Gloucestershire village compared notes and found out to their horror that each of their daughters had been 'ruined' by a man known only as 'Evil John' who hailed from the barren wastes of Shepherd's Bush. London always spelt trouble for toff stability; look at poor Mark Birley! Named a London nightclub after his wife and she bolted with that flashy little foreigner Jimmy

40

Diana in
her pram

Young Diana at Park
House

Diana with her brother
Charles

Diana as a young
adolescent

Early days in London
before the engagement

The balcony of Buckingham Palace after the wedding

Diana deep in conversation with Charles

Top: Diana greeting the crowds
Top Right: Charles
Above: A visit to Scotland
Right: Diana trying to evade the press

Top: With William after his concussion
Above: Visiting a leper hospital
Right: The school run
Below: Theme park fun with the boys

Diana, Harry, William and Charles

Diana wins the mother's race at Wetherby School, while
Charles trails badly behind in the father's race

Goldsmith! It is fear of the Evil Johns, and more covertly, of the Jimmy Goldsmiths, which leads upper-class parents to pay the earth to send their little darlings to all those finishing schools hidden away in the sterile mountains of Switzerland, with all that clean air and those same-sex dorms. But what begins as an effort to protect them actually drives such girls mad, and makes London in all its dirt and bustle seem all the more fascinating.

London has changed a great deal since Diana first came, saw and later conquered it two decades ago; the state of the upper-class girl has changed in particular. The streets of Fulham and Chelsea, which once rang with the braying neighs of Sloanes drinking at the Admiral Cod, now wince from the keening squeals of the trust-fund babes networking at the Beach. Once, when Diana was a girl – and how sad that phrase sounds now, how chill and historic, like 'When Victoria was a girl' – she and her friends wore Laura Ashley and Burberry and woollies from Warm And Wonderful; the designer labels came later, when she was a grown woman and an international icon. But Laura Ashley is gone now, every last sprigged skirt burned on the bonfire of the vanities where the upper class and the International White Trash – who had always shared SW London, but rarely mingled – met, exchanged prisoners and phone numbers and danced around each others' handbags. The simple fact is that life for an upper-class young Englishwoman was so boring, so soul-destroying, so stupidly sexist that at the first sign of interest from the IWT, they were off, pie-crust frills flouncing with fervour. It always took so little to entice these girls away, if the truth be told; a handful of crystals, a man in uniform, a blue plastic pyramid, a yacht in the Med, a place in the sun. All the might and patriarchy of the English class system – all brought down by a few flashy baubles dangled before the eyes of their womenfolk. Begging the question; what can it all have been worth in the first place?

If a girl becomes a debutante now, chances are that she will not be upper class as we understand the term at all but rather from a family in trade, a foreigner, or bearing a family name featuring an X or a Z – all well and good on an optician's chart but not so hot on the dotted line. Diana was never a debutante; her family was too grand and the idea of curtsying to a cake (which became the coming-out custom when the Queen refused to have debutantes presented to her in the 1950s) after spending a childhood sharing her family's swimming pool with the younger princes would have seemed frankly silly.

Girls who would once have been Sloanes now see how vapid and boring it all was, and have embraced the flashy, trashy habits of the International White Trash (what used to be called the Jet Set) during the week, while returning to Hampshire home and hearth – as in the case of Prince Charles' friend Tara Palmer-Tompkinson – at weekends. The IWT are vapid too in their (high) fashion, but they do appear to be having *fun*, and more to the point, the young women involved are never expected to defer to the young men as they were on the Sloane/deb circuit. In fact the trust-fund babes are good examples of Girl Power run riot, every one a little princess and having the time of their lives. Whereas upper-class women have been traditionally self-deprecating and self-sacrificing, these girls glory in their indulgence; 'Children smear chocolate over themselves and touch your things, don't they? I'm just too selfish to have a child,' said the heiress Tamara Beckwith memorably on why she gave her daughter to her mother to bring up.

The change that has taken place in the outlook of upper-class women, even over the past twenty years, can be seen in the respective social diaries of *Harpers & Queen*'s Jennifer and of the *Sunday Times'* Tara. While of lower social origin than Tara, Jennifer would never have countenanced Trade, let alone Showbiz in her diary; an occasion was made perfect only by the presence of 'our wonderful Queen' or 'the glorious Queen Mother', as late as 1978 when Diana Spencer made her wondering arrival in the capital. Tara, on the other hand, borrows her designer clothes in return for being photographed in fashionable nightspots in them, has taken money for promoting sunglasses and can write with not a hint of embar-rassment (not on her part, anyway) that 'Richard Branson invited me to a private party, along with Des Lynam and Chris Eubank, to celebrate the launch of his new cosmetics venture', and can drool after the cast of *EastEnders* (who seem to take a piquant pleasure in snubbing her whenever the opportunity arises) 'I'm their biggest fan'.

Things are swervy, nervy and topsy-turvy when it comes to class these days. In *Vanity Fair* a bevy of blue-blooded models – Stella Tennant, Honor Fraser, Jasmine Guinness – pose by Buckingham Palace wearing corsets, fishnets and punk eye

Diana

makeup, sticking their tails and tongues out, common as muck; on the cover of society magazine *Tatler* (edited by a Purley girl, of all things) pouts Victoria Adams, alias Posh Spice, daughter of a suburban electrician. What common Posh Spice and the posh totty have in common is that they are all self-made women; posh or not never came into it. In Diana's day, things were different.

Diana returned from Switzerland into a social scene in which the *wayang* shadow play could clearly be seen slinking slowly but surely towards its conclusion. Diana was a bridesmaid in the April of 1978 to her sister Jane, who was marrying Robert Fellowes, the Queen's private secretary, thus re-establishing the Spencers as part of the courtier class. Women of the Bedchamber, too; her sister Sarah was by then the girlfriend of the Prince of Wales. By the November of that year, Prince Charles invited Sarah Spencer, no longer his girlfriend, to his thirtieth birthday party. He asked Diana, too. By now, there was a feeling of horse-fancying about the annual inspection of Diana by the Prince's camp – expertly overseen by the Queen Mother and Lady Fermoy – checking her out every so often to see how she was shaping up. Or, more sinisterly, like the old witch in *Hansel and Gretel*, demanding that Hansel stick his arm through the bars of his cage every day, so she'll know when he's plump and juicy enough to enjoy.

By this time Diana was living in London, at her mother's flat in Cadogan Square. She lived the Sloane life supreme, simple to the point of being mind-boggling to a modern girl.

She once more went through the Marie Antoinette-menial routine, hiring herself out through various agencies as a cook, nanny, au pair and cleaner. She had little money, but she barely needed it, living as she did the life of a demobbed nun. She was a dreamy and somewhat self-loathing girl; just the type of upper-class flawed Meissen – from Caroline Lamb to Marianne Faithfull – who tends to jump feet first into whatever sort of silky oblivion is available under the benediction of the bright lights of the big city. But her life as an independent young woman, free for the first time to do as she pleased, was almost eerily wholesome and cloistered. Almost as though she knew what was ahead.

She read, watched television and went out to supper with her friends from school, spending her weekends at Althorp or at house parties with her girlfriends. She loved *Crossroads*, shepherd's pie, bacon sandwiches, Twiglets, Capital Radio, Miss Dior, Opal Fruits, wine gums. Her delight in passing for normal – not as a Spencer, not as the child of a famous divorce, not as 'Thicky' Spencer who failed her O Levels twice – can easily be imagined. In addition, she was becoming beautiful; photographs of the time show a smooth-haired, big-eyed, well-nourished girl of the English type traditionally called 'comely', and which men across all the classes – with the exception of the IWT – have such a weakness for. Her face was the presexual face of a medieval page, and the high necks and ruffles she often wore seemed to refer discreetly to her lineage.

Her quiet 'tidy' life seems to have pleased her intensely. For a girl of her age, she seemed to show a singular lack of interest in the seeking of excitement. Almost as if she knew that this was the only quiet time she would ever have again, and wanted to make the best of it. Her happiness was enhanced in the July of 1979 when, at last eighteen, her parents presented her with a £60,000 apartment in Coleherne Court. In an unknowing tribute to her chastity and to the desirability of keeping it that way, the flat was not in the Sloane heartland of Fulham and Kensington but in London's first gay village, Earl's Court.

It is often poignant and strange to think that, in the past, we may often have passed those we now love on the street, and never seen the face that was to become our Open Sesame of happiness. As the clean-cut, chubby young girl skittered through the streets of Earl's Court on her way to the latest cleaning job, eyes down, in her starched white blouses and full skirts, it is strange to think that she passed men, then healthy, who within the decade would come to see her as their very own Princess, the Princess of compassion who sat on their beds and held their hands and watched over them as they lay dying from the big disease with the little name.

Carolyns, Annes, Philippas, Sophies and Virginias came to stay. At this time, the girls in the flat attracted a great many boys. Nevertheless, it is true to say that these boys were far keener on Diana than she was on them; she made this up to them, in a very working-class, almost motherly way, by doing their washing and ironing. Sexual desire was simply not on her agenda; possibly due to the havoc she had watched it wreak at first hand. The Morton tapes have her speaking enigmatically but cheerfully of the occasion when Prince Charles first tried it on, as they sat on a bale of hay at a barbecue and she told him how sorry she felt for him after the killing of Lord Mounbatten; 'The next minute he leapt on me practically and I thought this was very strange too. Frigid wasn't the word. Big F when it comes to that.'

The Prince of Wales had no such finer feelings. He was already, you feel, by this time very probably a sex addict, though not in a happy way. Anyone who knows the first thing about sex knows that, along with other things, people search between the sheets for things they mislaid in their childhood (maybe they should look under the bed instead). In Prince Charles' case, it was obviously physical affection and tactile warmth, the lack of which coming from any parental direction probably qualified him as a man with a case for cruel and unusual punishment before he was out of short trousers. Anyone who has seen the famous Pathé newsreel of the young Queen returning from a long tour of duty only to *shake the hand* of the tiny boy who waits for her at the quayside will find it hard to forget or forgive.

When Diana Spencer, already an instinctive mother at the age of nineteen, told the Prince that he was lonely and needed someone to look after him, his first reaction was to leap on her; he already sensed the comfort she could bring him, but could express his gratitude only gropingly. In later years, when the marriage was capsizing, the Prince's camp would insinuate that it was Diana's simpering immaturity, her preference for pop over Wagner, which had driven the first bolster between them. But it seems likely that, emotionally, she was the senior partner, the guiding light from the word go.

Mrs Patrick Campbell's famous line about the allure of marriage – 'the comfort of the double bed after the hurly-burly of the chaise longue' – must also have played its part. The royal lunge took place in the July of 1980; at the end of 1979, the Prince had fallen under the spell of Anna 'Whiplash' Wallace, a reference both to her hard hunting habits and her sarcastic tongue. Worldly and wilful, she continued to provoke and evade him; it was around this time that the Prince told a biographer that he 'fell in love easily'; no 'Whatever love is' *there*, interestingly – until at a ball to celebrate the Queen Mother's eightieth birthday she yelled at him 'Don't ignore me like that again. I've never been treated so badly in my life! No one treats me like that – not even you!' Here was one Saracen princess who was a bit too hot to handle, obviously, even if she did come from Scotland.

Never very clever at taking a warning from a woman – he would lose Camilla Shand to another man, and lose his wife to the newspapers because he failed to take their threats seriously – within a few months he was left dancing in the dark with Mrs Parker-Bowles when Anna Wallace fled the scene of the thought-crime and burned rubber all the way to the altar with some other toff in possession of less money but more moxie. It was a very flighty, very eighties episode of the Royal soap opera, and can only have hastened the day Prince Charles finally felt it appropriate to settle down.

Camilla was married, but there was Diana – on standby for the past three years, simmering on a low heat, coming along nicely. The one he had made earlier would always be the only one to satisfy his appetite, but the dish of the day was moving up the menu fast – and the reviews were great. The marriage may well have been 'pretty crowded', as Diana was to say on *Panorama*, but it was more than just an infernal triangle. It was, rather, a double date; Charles and Camilla vs Diana and the Fourth Estate. They discovered her, nurtured her, chronicled her and buried her. They alone were faithful unto death; her face never fading into familiarity for them, and they never, ever wanted anyone else.

If only her husband could have said the same.

Always

and F

orever

The Royal Romance; the Fairytale Wedding

Chapter 3

Diana

As it was, things had a distinct whiff of panic buying. Operating in tried-and-trusted foot-in-mouth mode, the Prince of Wales once opined (and opining is definitely the word; that appalling blend of pomposity and insecurity which has combined to make him one of the most unprepossessing public speakers in Britain today) that thirty was the perfect age for a man to marry. In the summer of 1980 he was thirty-two and still living at home with his mother, albeit a very liberal-minded mother who did not object to him bringing girls back. This courtesy even extended to the actress Susan George who Charles, rather rudely, had taken a shine to after seeing her (or rather, as it transpired, her body double) being gang-raped in the film *Straw Dogs*. Obviously one of the perks of being the Prince of Wales was being able to enjoy a Royal Command Performance in the privacy of one's own bedroom. Despite the repeated bleatings of the geek chorus of Windsor-brown-nosers who argue that being royal is a dog's life, it would appear that this dog was well and truly having his day. A cosy central London pad, a stream of hot and cold running blondes delivered to the door, polo on Saturdays and a sure billet for the future.

Prince Charles' single state was like a Rorschach test; everyone saw in it what they wanted to see. His father saw yet another example of his son's dithering nature and a great excuse to bully him even further. The Queen Mother saw yet more proof that the Prince needed minding – and she knew just the Woman of the Bedchamber to do it. The country saw yet another instance of an uncharismatic, directionless member of a family they were growing increasingly impatient with, who seemed to have turned loafing into a fine art. And the Queen? The Queen, as ever, through a combination of embarrassment and guilt, simply saw no evil.

Prince Charles had spent his life being someone's son; a vital part in making him grow up in the eyes of the people he one day hoped to reign over was to turn him into a husband. By this time, any idea that he might want to wait until he fell in love again was rapidly losing ground. This was the family, let us not forget, who called itself the Firm – a typical Dukism, implying dynamism and the patrician nose to the grindstone to conceal a life largely composed of Awaydays at home, holidays abroad, playing with dogs and betting on horses. It stood to reason that a marriage would be more of a merger than normally thought desirable, and the ideal candidate one who should appeal to the public more than to the Prince himself. Someone young, someone sweet and, above all, someone who could breed the children which the exhausted and unpopular Windsors could hold up to the revolting peasants outside the gates of Buck House and batter them back into submission with a huge collective 'AHHHH'! And as it turned out, everyone got what they wanted – at least for a while. The Duke, the Prince, the Queen Mother, Lady Fermoy, the country. Everyone, of course, except the bride.

When working-class or middle-class men and women marry, they tend to marry for the same reason; love. Alongside this there is a sense that other things are almost as vital; friendship,

Diana

shared aspirations and the ability to have sex five times a day. The upper-class man and woman are not similarly well suited. Upper-class women, as we have seen, receive an education barely fit for a five-year-old child (Queen Mary, the most serious member of the Royal Family, was forever sweeping into the schoolroom of the young Princesses Elizabeth and Margaret and demanding that their governess give them a proper education), and so at puberty the idea of Love spreads, like horse manure, to cover the stable floor where elements such as career, ideas and ambition should be gaining ground.

But the upper-class man is certainly not raised to believe that love is the pinnacle of human existence. Brought up largely separated from their mothers, boys are drilled in the dry rituals of duty; to estate, country and the hereditary principle. Love and marriage may well go together like a horse and carriage for many; but for the average upper-class man, they are about as likely a coupling as a fish and a rickshaw. So by this time it is entirely likely that Prince Charles had decided to lie back and enjoy it (whatever 'it' means. . .). For once in his life he knew what it felt like to be a hounded, hunted thing, his family and the country and the courtiers all baying for his hand to be given in marriage to the swiftest galloping girl, just as the brush of the fox is given to the bravest hunter. Whether Diana was the hunted or hunter is a question which has come up at many points in her life; with the gentlemen of the press, with James Hewitt, with fame and of course during the open season on the Prince of Wales' solo state. Physically, the looks of both hunted and hunter were part of what made her so

54

immediately attractive to everyone. But strangely, it was when she was the hunter than she looked like the hunted – with her wide Disney eyes, trembling lips, shy mute smile and scuttling run – and when she became the hunted creature of later legend then she really came to look like Diana the Huntress; all burnished golden hair, strong striding legs and tanned, toned arms just made to hold a bow and arrow.

It would be fair to say that at this point she was 'after' him, but she was less chasing him deliberately than following him helter-skelter like one runaway train after another or like a whippet chasing a clockwork rabbit. By this time her vista was limited to the tunnel vision caused by the betrayal of both her body and mind; her dream of dancing squeezed out by her beautiful tallness and her chance of a career killed by the fact that her spirit and imagination had been stunted by the dullest of educations. Even 'Thicky' Spencer had got the message by now; she was meant to get married. If that was to be so, then she would make her marriage her career and her art and her everything. She would make a real marriage, one not based on incubation and in-fighting and she would recreate a family from the ashes of Althorp. She would do her best, despite her husband's hungry heart and she would vow it to her country in front of the world.

Later, when she realized that her marriage was going the way of her parents' marriage, and that, worst of all, her beloved boys would now feel as she had felt, as her younger brother had felt when he cried for his mother at night and Diana was too frightened of the dark to go and comfort him,

Diana

her feelings of panic and grief can only be guessed at. Later, when she was sure she knew why everything was falling apart – that her husband had finally followed his heart all the way back to his leathery 'lady', as Diana sadly called her towards the end – it would have been enough to drive a weaker woman mad. Shamefully, the Prince's courtiers would grasp at her confusion with indecent haste and eagerness and explain that she was not right in the head. As a combination of Kafka and *Gaslight*, it was perhaps one of the ugliest cases of marital mental torment to come to light this side of Oprah.

Diana was a pretty, prancing pony; she had to be broken in by the Firm, and she had to be put through her paces. The final jump and the highest one was Balmoral, where Diana met her fate; the shameless paired circles of ground glass peering across the River Dee at her.

Now everyone was hooked. The press were on her trail, and on her return to London they followed, rats deserting the drab Family Windsor in order to follow this page-boyed Pied Piper back to a capital that she would never see in the same way again. London had represented an anonymous, independent life to Diana, a place where she could eat Twiglets, scrub floors and play at being normal. Now her cover had been blown. Once the children at her school had pointed because only her parents were divorced; now Diana would only see London again through a mass of pointing cameras and binoculars and microphones, pointing not because of a divorce but because of a marriage. The city she had known disappeared before her eyes like a mirage; in its place lay a long, winding catwalk on which she would be expected to parade a never-ending succession of gorgeous gowns and sunny smiles. Her long, sad journey along the Yellow Brick Road of celebrity had begun.

She was alone from the beginning. When she asked Buckingham Palace what she should do, they told her it was none of their business. Reporters phoned her all night and chased her red Mini Metro all day. In the naive belief that if she gave them what they wanted they would stop wanting it, Diana posed for the press outside the Young England kindergarten where she was working, holding one child in her arms and the other by the hand. Her skirt against the sun was transparent and the first iconic image of Diana was produced; sweet docile face, a way with children and legs like expressways to delirium. It was to become the most famous leg shot since Marilyn Monroe stood over the grating and gloried in the cold. Hurtfully, in a way that was to become a habit and which can have done no good whatsoever to an insecure girl on the verge of believing she was too fat, Prince Charles delivered a caress-kick comment by telling her that he hadn't realized she had such great legs – and did she really have to show them to the world? When she wore the famous low-cut black dress to meet Princess Grace, her breasts would come in for the same treatment. It was, in a surreal *Psycho* way, as though the personalities of his parents were warring within the Prince; the Mother who was benign and the Father who was bellicose. It must have already been getting mighty crowded in there.

sweet docile face, a way with children and legs like expressways to delirium

Only one person helped her; Shy Di. Shy Di was, in a way, the imaginary friend Lady Diana Spencer, complex and self-possessed, made up to help her through this difficult time, just as 'Thicky' Spencer had helped her through her dismal school-days. The name Diana seemed somehow unsuitable for her as the nation fell in love; 'Diana' was hard-edged and flighty, be she Diana Cooper, Diana Mitford or Diana Dors. So it was 'Shy Di' who skittered to her car in the morning, peeping out from under her fringe as the press corps moved with her along the street to her car, already almost like a royal guard. She had smooth hair then and sturdy legs under full skirts; she was, above all, 'tidy'. She looked like what Anthony Burgess called 'an icon of cleanliness' in a dirty world.

But below the skittering and blushes, there were already signs that this was no ordinary nineteen-year-old. She had a way of looking up at the press as she fumbled with her car keys and they pressed their questions upon her, a look which some people described as 'demure' because her eyes were big and her mouth was silent. But her eyes said more; there was a taunt in them, almost, which seemed to say 'I know something you don't know'. This could have been 'I know you love me' or even 'I know he doesn't love me'. But whatever it was, her shyness seemed distinctly like a disguise.

And she had quite a lot to hide, this virgin bride. Ironically, as she had once had to suffer singling out because of the sexual conduct of her parents, she was now keeping another dirty little secret which, if it came out, would shame her even though she herself had never acquired carnal knowledge. (She probably thought it was a section in Trivial Pursuit.) For the ghost of Camilla Parker-Bowles – often laid, but still impossible to exorcize once and for all – had re-emerged, her photographs falling out of books, her jewellery still burning a hole in the pockets of that Prince of Wales check, her sexual favours dispensed upon the royal train (when, hilariously, a *Sunday Mirror* reporter mistook her for Diana), her unheard voice on the other end of the phone as Diana listened outside doors to hear her fiancé say 'Whatever happens I will always love you' to someone else. It was the stuff of soap opera, of a million bad episodes of *Crossroads* that Diana must have laughed through with her flatmates. Now it was a joke to which she was the punchline. And being a punchline is probably the loneliest place of all.

Like the poor lost Cockney woman in the old music hall song, the Prince dillied and dallied, he dallied and he dillied, lost his way and didn't know where to go. From the *Sun* headline of 8 September 1980 – 'HE'S IN LOVE AGAIN! Lady Di is the new

Diana

girl for Charles' – to the engagement announcement of 24
February 1981, Prince Charles kept moving in a blizzard of
displacement activity. He toured India, relaxed in Nepal,
trekked through the Himalayas and skiied in Switzerland
while Diana ran a daily gauntlet. It was the first time he made
it clear that he would never be there for her and he never was;
not at their concussed son's bedside, not at the Taj Mahal, not
at heart. When we watch film of that gorgeous, Godforsaken
wedding which took place that day in July 1981, it comes as a
surprise to see two people standing at the altar, making vows
of eternal love, promising in the sight of God to honour and
cherish. Three people, yes; one person, perhaps. But there
were never two. We simply saw what we wanted to see.

And we wanted to see her. We had seen her blush, smile,
run, drive and swear when her car wouldn't start. It was hope-
less and we were all helpless. We weren't really sure any more
if the monarchy was a good thing or a bad thing for this country, but such grown-up grumbles melted like meringue in our
mouths when we beheld her. We just wanted to look at her
forever, and we would never stop.

Prince Charles, always a man to choose the softer of two
soft options, had had enough. The country approved, his
family approved, the press approved and, most importantly of
course, Camilla approved. It was only a matter of time before
he popped, in the breezy, chilling Sloane vernacular, the question. But the question was not what this trusting and vulnerable young woman needed. She needed an answer, more than
anything in the world; the answer to her fear that he was in

love with someone else. Rather than telling her on the telephone that he had something to ask her when he came home, he should have had something to tell her; that he was in love with someone else, always had been and always would be, and that what he understood as marriage was the traditional upper-class model of wife and mistress pulling as a team. But no one seemed to want the truth when the lie was so sweet. It was Truth or Dare; he chose the Dare. That night at Windsor Castle when the Truth was put on ice and the Dare pulled from its velvet box, imagine what a wonderful, terrible sight she must have been; that sad girl, with all that pain and rejection behind her, telling him over and over how much she loved him as affection swooshed out of her like a firework from a bottle. Irresistible, really, to all but one. Having finished telling him how she felt, she stopped and waited for him to say those three little words. And he said them.

'Whatever love means. . .'

Prince Charles seemed fond of these words. He would say them again on television on the day the engagement was announced, so that 500 million people could hear them, look at their companions, raise their eyebrows in wonder and then shrug guiltily, washing it from their hands with a silent acknowledgement that the Royals are just *different* from us. This gauche girl, so luminously happy in a cheap-looking blue suit and an expensive-looking blue ring, was a reproach in the face of our cynicism. She wanted to believe. And, in the manner of children willing Tinker Bell not to die, we closed our eyes and murmured yes, we do, we do, we do believe in fairies. Four months after the first sighting of her, what the biddies of the Bedchamber had brought into being the gentlemen of the press finessed. Their very own Pygmalion did them proud, never flinching or looking back when the bodyguards came for her in the dead of night, as if for a political prisoner, the night before the engagement was announced.

It was the coldness that struck Diana about the family she was about to marry into. Perhaps big houses make families as chill as their many rooms and corridors have a habit of being, and only being cramped together forces human beings to rub along in any sort of humour and harmony. One imagines lots of walking away within the House of Windsor, and with all those homes – Buckingham, Balmoral, Sandringham, Windsor – with all those rooms, it must be very easy for families never to need to thrash their problems out. At Clarence House and then at Buckingham Palace a few days later, Diana was given rooms and the servants became her family, waking and feeding and dressing her. At times, the grandeur and the chill and the very obvious absence of a beloved face – a house is not a home! – must have made it feel like her sad and empty Norfolk home after her mother left. Once again, she must have wondered what she was being punished for.

She wore a black dress, That Black Dress, for her first official engagement, which now seems highly suitable. For even as Diana moved irrevocably towards her marriage, she was mourning her one real romance, which now that she had been hooked, reeled in and weighed seemed effectively over. When

I think of this time I think of an old American pop song from the seventies called 'The Days Of Pearly Spencer' which goes, in part, like this:

You played the House that can't be beat, now look, your head bowed in defeat/You walked too far along the street where only rats can run/Ah, the days of Pearly Spencer/Ah, the race is almost run. . .

Now she really was alone. Whatever the insecurities that had racked her childhood, turning her into a strange little girl, as the most interesting little girls always are, very young – her brother Charles recalled to Andrew Morton the time when the local Norfolk vicar's wife stopped the school run car and said 'Diana Spencer, if you tell one more lie like that I will make you walk home' – her independent life as a young working woman, such as it was, had managed to draw her back down to earth. All that ironing and cooking and cleaning and bringing up baby, all those things that drive most women mad, had been the agents of her first therapy, grounding techniques that left her too preoccupied and then too tired to think weird thoughts. In another life – born into a lower class, where she might have been given a decent education – she might have been a Nicola Horlick, burping babies and closing deals with equal enthusiasm and energy.

But her sad upbringing had led her to this lonely place and now everyone involved in her evolution seemed to believe that she should be over the moon. Most upper-class girls

Diana

thought of a good match as being someone with a fair-sized country house and a soft billet in the City. She had landed the Prince of Wales. Yet it was a squeegee, not a sceptre, she longed for, and only the servants she could talk to. But like any woman who has worked for a living and is then deprived of that work, depression was now her shadow, standing between her and the sun when she awoke each morning and reading over her shoulder by candlelight each night. It is to be wondered if she still read her Barbara Cartland novels about young virgins being swept away by dashing men in uniform. Or if she by now had moved on to something escapist.

Detective stories, perhaps. From inside the belly of the beast, it was easier to find out exactly what was going on between her fiancé and his mistress. She followed up many leads and they all ended in tears. It was the treasure hunt from Hell: bracelets and cufflinks exchanged between the gruesome twosome uncovered; and photographs of Camilla fell out of his diary on that same honeymoon. You sometimes wonder whether Charles was ever tempted after one glass of cherry brandy too many to offer Diana a pair of riding boots, a hard hat and a Halloween mask and ask her to go all the way towards fulfilling his fantasy of being with the woman he loved.

As the wedding approached and Diana was seen in tears at airports seeing him off on tours, on polo fields watching him play and at wedding rehearsals looking at him practise his lying, the first great blame-shifting attempts took place on the part of the Palace, which pleaded with the media to let her

alone. In truth, though, it was being left alone by her fiancé
and his family as this massive event came at her like a screech-
ing banshee of a railway train – and she the innocent girl tied
to the tracks as in a silent movie – that made her cry like that.
It was not the barbarians at the gates; it was the enemy within.

It was not the barbarians at the gates; it was the enemy within

If you're going to tell a lie, be sure you make it a big one. While
you're at it, why not go the whole hog and tell it to seven
hundred million people in seventy-four countries all around
the world. Tell it in St Paul's Cathedral and take seventy-five
minutes to tell it. Then sell videos of it. Make it the Taj Mahal
of lies.

Spend millions of pounds on the setting for your lie. As this
was a wedding totally to do with pragmatism and protocol
and nothing to do with love, it had to be as fancy and fussy as
possible, just so the cracks wouldn't show through. It is odd;
when the poverty and deprivation of the most vulnerable
members of our society raise their hideous Hydra heads in yet
another new report – the number of children living below the
poverty line, the number of old people dying of hypothermia
– we are invariably told that throwing money at the problem

Diana

won't cure it. But money spent on state occasions is never missed. This is indeed the logic of the lunatic asylum; that it is not done to apply money to problems, but to parties instead. Pomp, ceremony and pageantry – we do it so well! Our island story – let the bells ring out! Unclean, unclean – that's what the bells should have said.

The bride was very beautiful, half a foot smaller around the waist than she had been when she first caught the camera's eye that day by the River Dee, thanks to the bulimia she had picked up at the Palace – what, this little thing? I've had it for years! – as her unhappiness over the antics of Fred and the whip-thin Gladys lassooed and corralled her. She was frail and pale in her highly defined Barbara Daly makeup, the loveliest she had ever looked, and this was a good thing because somehow a bride who is not beautiful makes a big white wedding look faintly grotesque and comic – like those cardboard cut-outs of fat people at the seaside that you can stick your head through. We had seen this before with the wedding of Princess Anne, and would see it again with the nuptials of Sarah Ferguson. Diana was not just a bride, she was *The Bride*, as in 'Here Comes The. . .' or as in the film title *The Princess Bride*. We had all seen a wagonload of brides in white before we saw her; after her, every white-clad bride seems to be Diana, in all her doomed glory. She simply made the part hers – like Sean Connery and James Bond. She was perfect.

But little things mean a lot and looking back it is grimly satisfying to notice that there were odd little glitches that glinted sharply from this sumptuous smorgasbord of self-congratulation on the part of the House of Windsor. The dress, by David and Elizabeth Emanuel, who would divorce within the decade, was not traditional white but ivory, on the grounds that it would televise better. (So would Prince Andrew's head on Prince Charles' shoulders just for the day, as Adrian Mole pointed out in his diary, but no one bothered with that.) The ivory looked slightly off, as though it had failed to be quite what it should be, which was appropriate. The train was too long to fit tidily into the Glass Coach which was to take her and her father to St Paul's and the whole twenty-five feet of it was visibly crushed as Diana made her way up the aisle in front of seven hundred million people. That should teach them not to show off, you couldn't help thinking. Twenty-five feet of train!

As for the poor Earl, he had troubles of his own. Very badly disabled and, to be brutal, stiff in all the wrong places ever since his stroke, he was nevertheless thrilled by the occasion and it is likely that his very excitement contributed to his obvious confusion. Knowing how Diana was already able to lose her own anxiety by focusing on the troubles of others instead, it is entirely likely that the calmness that she both showed and says she felt that day was hers by virtue of the fact that looking after her father took her mind off herself and what lay ahead.

But as the poor old man made his painfully slow progress down the great length of the aisle, we can only imagine what charitable thoughts were flitting idly through the minds of the Family Windsor as they observed him. For they are a family which enjoys rude health, and which has spent far too much

Diana

time around horses – poor fellow, shoot him and put him out of his misery – to think that a life less lived has anything at all to recommend it over a mercifully swift end. When sub-standard relatives refuse to do the decent thing and die, they simply lie about it; within the decade the existence would come to light of a pair of poor feeble-minded Bowes-Lyons cousins of the Queen Mother, mouldering in an institution. All well and good, since few of us would wish to care for the mentally ill ourselves these days, relations or not. But did the Royal Family really have to insist for years that they were both dead?

Earl Spencer certainly didn't look like a man proudly giving his daughter away, thrilled or not; the stroke made him seem both deadly slow and deadly scared, as though he would rather do anything than ever get her to the altar and hand her over to the enemy. It was a fluke, but with hindsight an eerie one; he had the aspect of a man accompanying his precious daughter – beautiful, light-hearted and unknowing of her fate – to the stake or to the guillotine.

Once they got to the altar, there were gaffes to delight the hearts of Light Entertainment archivists everywhere. The bride got the groom's name wrong, calling him Philip Charles Arthur George by mistake; 'She's married my father!' exclaimed Prince Andrew, who, of course, as Adrian Mole had said, should have been up there at the Princess Bride's side in the first place – a natural king, good-natured, medium-dull and decidely untortured, with, as it turned out, a nice line in loyalty to his wife (even that wife) as opposed to his family.

What are we to make of Diana's slip at this most vital of moments, after all those rehearsals? Well, let us not forget that she often spoke of her psychic abilities; it may well have drifted into her unconscious that Prince Philip had been pushing for this match with a good deal more enthusiasm than his son had, and that in a way the impulse which had brought her there was his – like a spirit guide or Sherpa Tensing taking the Brits up Everest. As for the Prince himself and knowing what a tormented relationship he has with his father, I am sure it has not been beyond him, his lackeys and Sir Laurens van der Post to come up with some wacky theory about how Diana's covert madness and hostility sought to castrate him on the altar of his own wedding in front of the world, his wife and their witchdoctor by taking Philip Charles Arthur George as her wedded husband rather than his son the sap.

The second dud to hit the deck was the worldly goods, a not inconsiderable amount on this outing. Was he still thinking about what a cow Diana was to want to marry his father when the Prince spitefully offered; 'And all thy goods with thee I share' instead of 'And all my worldly goods with thee I share'? ('That was no mistake!' said Princess Anne.) It was true that he had a reputation for stinginess and he may well have presumed that as his heart was on a long lease elsewhere the marriage might one day run into trouble. But that really was leaving the pre-nuptial agreement somewhat late in the day.

The Archbishop of Canterbury told us that this was the stuff of which fairytales are made and he never said a truer word. The Queen looked very solemn, as well she might. The

Diana

assembly sang 'I Vow To Thee My Country', Diana's favourite hymn, which looking back sounds like the first revving of rebellion; a country is more than its monarchy, and the heart of that country can be led astray onto the paths of righteousness, as she was to show. Camilla wore grey, the colour of moral relativism, as in 'Nothing is black and white, only shades of grey.' Then everyone went home.

The glitches were only small, of course. Anyone is allowed a few slip-ups on their big day. It was the other stuff that mattered. That the woman he loved was in the church, though not standing beside him, as he promised all manner of fantastic and unlikely things. And that it was all a pack of lies. How bitterly we look back now at the videos, the mugs, the commemorative plaques purchased with such coy and eager glee. How we were fooled! All of us plebs, drowning in our tears, strangulating on our bunting, choking on our wedding cake – talk about one born every minute!

the woman he loved was in the church, though not standing beside him

And we know, of course, that Marshal Stalin was wrong when he had the faces of all those who had displeased him literally blacked out of the history books, and later expertly painted over so they just disappeared. But it would be lovely if by magic we could go back to those videos and mugs and commemorative plaques and just get rid of him, of his mother, of the whole lousy lot of them. And have it just as her, on her perfect day, when she married all of us, like at one of those mass Moonie weddings.

Just her, standing there shining and waving and drowning, seeming to be the start of something new. What, we didn't yet know. But for the moment, for that day, that would do.

Don't you

want me?

And the truth about that marriage

Chapter **4**

Diana

If Diana Spencer, a twenty-year-old virgin bride, had ever had any doubts as to her physical attractiveness and ability to drive her new husband wild with desire, they must have been swept away like confetti in a Force 10 gale when, in front of 60,000 of Her Majesty's cheering subjects, the following exchange took place on the balcony of Buckingham Palace:

Crowd: Kiss her! Kiss her!
Prince Andrew: Give her a kiss.
Prince Charles: I'm not getting into that caper.
Prince Andrew: Give her a kiss!
Prince Charles (to Queen): May I?
Queen: Yes.

Yes, it was Mr Whatever-Love-Means up to his old tricks again; throwing a wet blanket over the proceedings, bringing the party down, putting his foot in his mouth and generally upsetting everyone, especially his young wife. The Kiss, as it came to be called (probably in the singular because it was the only one we ever expected him to give her on the mouth), photographed well; she may have gone a long way towards losing her formerly robust health during the trials of the engagement, but she had gained the neck of a swan and the camera loves one of these. Even Prince Charles looked alright; you couldn't see his face, for a start.

The couple cut the five-foot-tall wedding cake (a tricky manoeuvre, this, considering how close it stood to the short, round Queen Mother in her usual sugared-almond finery) with Prince Charles' sword (nice to see it out to some practical use for a change) which included so many cherries, sultanas, raisins and currants that it had taken four men two days to pip and stalk them (the phrase 'No job for a man' inevitably comes to mind here). In place of the usual weather-house figurines of a man and a woman, the cake featured coloured icing pictures of the bride's and groom's family crests, coats of arms and stately homes. The ability of the upper classes yet again to rival the rawest monster-mawed new rich yuppie in vulgar dumb show was displayed nicely here; while they were at it, why didn't they go the whole hog and ice on the bank balances of both families, too? Probably because there was no cake big enough to do the Windsors' family fortune justice.

The new Princess of Wales changed into a pink silk going-away number by Bellville Sassoon; both larky and elegant, with something non-specifically defiant about the hat, it was the first signal of her own unique style, slippery and elegant and just this side of vulgar, as she broke free from the stifling sweetness of Sloanedom. It was pink, but not baby pink or cosy pink; pink as coral, of the type that looks beautiful from a distance but if you dare to grasp, it breaks off in your flesh, leaving its stinging spines beneath the skin, and hurts you horribly.

So there they were: JUST MARRIED. In fact, ONLY JUST MARRIED might have been a better banner. Prince Charles later said that on the eve of the wedding he had watched from the Palace as 'all night people were sitting out on the steps there singing "Rule Britannia" and every kind of thing. . .I found myself standing in the window with tears pouring down my face'. What a pair; they'd spent the night before their wedding not gleefully and drunkenly fornicating (with each other), as sensible, romantic people do; instead, she'd spent it vomiting and he weeping. Now wasn't that a dainty dish to put before the Queen.

You could see that she and the Duke, like their son, were more than anything relieved that it was all over. And that is why a cynic should never marry an idealist. For the cynic, marriage represents the welcome end of romantic life, with all its agony and ecstasy. But for the idealist, it is only the beginning.

They started their honeymoon at Broadlands, where Mountbatten had lived – and which, as Denholm Elliott's evil Dr Swabey says in *A Private Function*, sounds unfortunately like a mental institution. The Queen and Prince Philip had spent the first few days of their honeymoon there too so, conveniently, the Prince of Wales could consult with his mother's spirit presence if ever he felt moved to ask permission to kiss his wife again.

He fished for salmon; she fished for compliments. Then they set sail on the royal yacht *Britannia* for the Mediterranean. In many ways it had been an arranged marriage, and to a woman raised on romance, the honeymoon must have signalled the winning tape and starting blocks both, when the veil could be drawn aside and the curtains closed to create a cocoon of pure Cartlandian bliss. But rather reminiscent of the old music hall song 'And Her Mother Came Too', they were surrounded by twenty-one officers and two hundred and fifty-six ordinary sailors.

It is sad to conclude that one of the things which probably did attract Prince Charles about Lady Diana Spencer was not her untouched nubility but something which reflects even more malignly upon a man of his age; what he perceived as her ignorance. It was, indeed, 'Thicky' Spencer that he took rather a shine to. For while the truly clever feel no need to patronize others, the bogus intellectual will take any chance that comes to hand, real or imagined, to prove his superiority to the clod in the street. But very early on there were signs that Diana was far brighter, in all senses of the word, than her husband. She may have only received booby prizes at school for being Little Miss Sunshine, but then she received a shockingly bad education and was always *expected* to fail. But his truly bog-standard degree, after the best education money and rank could buy, could easily be seen as a cap-and-gown equivalent of the Best-kept Hamster.

During the press-gang drag-hunt of her engagement, Diana Spencer said 'Don't make me sound like a bookworm, because I'm not, but I'll read almost anything I can get my hands on, from women's magazines to Charles Dickens. I read because I enjoy it.' Generally, this attitude to books is found among the naturally bright – think of the true intellectual's enduring love for detective novels – rather than the phoney, adolescent cramming of Solzhenitsyn and Kafka which characterizes the Prince of Wales. Those aren't books you read; those are books you wear.

No, their IQs were always perfectly compatible; the big difference was that he was pretentious while she was not. And are we to totally go against the judgement God gave us and believe that a true intellectual seeking a soulmate would reject his young wife's company for Camilla Parker-Bowles and Dale Tryon? Please! That's rather like joining a Parchman Farm chain-gang in search of a slap-up lunch.

But innocent young creature as she was, she wanted to get to *know* him. And perhaps Prince Charles' self-awareness was in good working order in at least one department; perhaps he knew that *there wasn't a lot to get to know* – just a rather aimless and flighty and third-rate chap, born under a bad sign to fill a role which he had neither the desire nor the aptitude for. Just a hollow man with the worst job description on earth, waiting for his mother to die.

To fall in love is to offer your whole personality, your character, everything that made you, good and bad, to one other person. To offer that love on the understanding that that is what people do from a viewpoint of complete sexual and romantic innocence, and to see the expression on the face of the love object change to one of unmistakable appalled dismay must be a blow to one's self-esteem pretty much beyond the hope of recovery. The argument against library tickets for all can be made here; Prince Charles obviously so loved the works of Kafka that as a honeymoon treat he was making every attempt to recreate that nightmare world of imprisonment, false memory, paranoia and grand deception for his new bride, when she probably would have preferred a trip to Disneyland.

Deprived of any ordinary human comfort, Diana did what confused and powerless young women often do; she became bulimic. And because it was now her job, as surely as any supermodel, to have her photograph taken, and because during their engagement her fiancé had put his arm around her waist and commented on her chubbiness, she was making herself sick four times a day as the Love Boat cruised by Algeria, Tunisia, Sicily, the Greek islands, through the Suez Canal and the Red Sea and into Egypt, and between bouts of sunbathing, swimming, scuba-diving, snorkelling and windsurfing.

Here was the first sighting of the paradox that is heartbreak in luxury; when you are so very publicly doing the things that would make ordinary people happy, or so they believe, it is hard for a long time to show that you are actually in pain, for fear of seeming like that most pathetic of clichés – a poor little rich girl. So the more you do the things that comfort you as best they can – holidays in the sun, your picture in the *Sun*, a supermarket sweep all down South Molton Street with a diamond and platinum trolley – the more you make a rich little rod for your own suntanned back. Miserable, her? With that life? Look at her romp in the surf, dive from the yacht, dance with John Travolta! Bird in a gilded cage? Move over, Princess, and make mine mink!

She had wanted to be a dancer, she had shown great ability at working with children; but at the age of twenty vomiting

Diana

was her new vocation, and her vacation was arranged around it; four times a day, just like cleaning your teeth. Bulimia nervosa is a condition affecting thousands of sufferers in this country, nearly all of them female. It might well be called 'the caring disease' on two counts; that it disproportionately affects women in the 'caring' professions, who seeing self-sacrifice as the norm, come to translate their own basic needs and desires – for food, even – as greed and self-indulgence in desperate need of correcting through the penance of purgative medicine. And unlike its haughty older sister, anorexia, which screams its pain in people's faces and stares blank-eyed as the loved ones around it weep to see their little girl turning into an Oxfam poster right in front of them, bulimia tries to protect others, to pretend there's no problem. When men are angry and upset, they rebel by hurting others; when women are angry and upset, they rebel by hurting themselves; bulimia, anorexia, self-mutilation, suicide, getting married to members of the Windsor family. No wonder they didn't understand her illness; if she'd gone out and blasted a bit of wildlife to death, she'd most likely have felt all the better for it.

But that was not her way; she was, when all was said and done, a gentle creature. And like Dostoevsky's heroine, her gentleness went hand in hand with a spirited, high-stepping pride which, in the end, was to be her salvation. She would never throw herself out of a window clasping an icon because living had simply become impossible. But in those dark days on the Love Boat that never was, bulimia must have seemed both her lonely fate and guiding light; at last, something she could control.

After two weeks at sea they flew straight to Balmoral, where the mists and quiet, the shadows and fog made clear the awful mistake that the dazzle of the Med had done its best to keep at bay. Diana was, as returning brides from honeymoon are meant to be, exhausted. The difference was that this exhaustion came not from – nudge-nudge – looking at one too many bedroom ceilings but from looking at one too many bathroom floors.

She looked beautiful because she was as thin as she would ever be. And she looked thin because she was as sick as she would ever be, her body racked by the constant push and shove of bingeing and purging. When asked about her experience of married life on a photocall, she answered 'I can highly recommend it'. Like many sharing, caring bulimics, she was well on the way to becoming an excellent actress. For the curtain was up, the lights were lit and the show must go on.

It was a fairytale marriage, alright, from the word GO!, from the sign JUST MARRIED; a fairytale scripted by the Brothers Grimm, all locked rooms, icy-hearted queens and night starvation. That, or a version of *Cinderella* in which the unsuspecting, virtuous heroine is not plucked from isolation and cruelty as a reward for her beauty and purity, but rather condemned to it. Very soon – with the dry, self-mocking, very English wit which was to provide a welcome balance to her developing tendency to the occasional bout of damp,

Diana

self-dramatizing American therapy-speak – Diana was calling herself the Prisoner of Wales.

Coming from a broken home, yearning to create a real one, she was about to be treated by her husband and his parents – the mother so upright and dutiful, the father wearing all those medals – with a degree of manipulation which would have out-dazzled the dynasties of *Dallas*, the most popular programme of the day on television. We all know that the Queen's idea of heaven is supper on a tray in front of the telly – just like one of us, bless her, left to her own devices! – and it would not be too far-fetched to suggest that the family-managing machinations of that other sainted matriarch of a filthy rich and ever unruly family, Miz Ellie Ewing, held as strong a sway over the Queen as the back-to-the-land green dreams of Barbara Good. Yet from the scraps Diana was thrown, sitting there in her sumptuous scullery in her designer tatters, eating her tragic, nightly bowl of custard before going to her lonely bed, she made a life; a real, well-lived, well-used life in which she visibly pushed herself from bovine upper-class ignorance to a state of inquisitive, crusading sentience. And in getting herself a life – in wanting to know, in daring to look naive – she showed the House of Windsor up for what it was; a numb, dumb dinosaur, lumbering along in a world of its own, gorged sick on arrogance and ignorance.

Above all, she showed up her husband, the supposed 'intellectual' of the Firm, for what he was; a third-rate mind fronting a restless heart which signalled with every flinch, wince and *faux pas*, making it painfully obvious that he found it increasingly difficult either to love his people or do his duty. In fact, the Prince had, for a considerable time, seemed distinctly uncomfortable with anything on less than four legs or two knees. While no feminist radical, Diana was blessed with spirit – remember that she had refused to obey even at the altar – and it is entirely likely that the Prince of Wales, used to mistresses who called him 'Sir' in bed, registered this most attractive of qualities in a woman as out-and-out scrappiness. Before long he was turning to more compliant women for comfort of various kinds.

Prince Charles is apparently both emotionally inhibited and emotionally incontinent – pulling off this difficult trick probably being his greatest achievement in life so far. The Prince of Wales' notorious ability to blame others when things go wrong is well documented by those who have had the misfortune to work with him. This would seem to have extended to his marriage.

Balmoral is the most royal of the royal homes; the most remote, the most unknown, the place where the Royal Family can really unwind and be themselves – cold, snobbish and hide-bound by history. Buckingham Palace has somehow been made cheap and common enough to be regarded affection-ately by its permanent gaggle of Japanese tourists pressed up against the railings. Sandringham and Windsor feel Home Counties-cosy and have acquired a somewhat gruesome folksy air, due to the just-like-us sixties propaganda of the tele-vision documentary, *Royal Family*, and the tired old tales of the

Diana

Queen and Mrs Wilson sharing the washing-up duties after the Duke and Harold threw together an impromptu barbecue lunch. But Balmoral is the awful truth.

And at Balmoral, even more than at Broadlands or at sea, Diana realized the awful truth; that there were three of them in the marriage, as she would testify later in her cathode-ray confessional. Not just that, but *they didn't want her*, didn't want her in Queen Victoria's chair or anywhere in their precious Family. This was the second family she'd seen slip away from her in only twenty years; to lose one family might be an accident; to lose two must mean she had done something really bad.

She had never thought much of herself; she had certainly not approached the family she married into with a 'hello-fans, get-me' kind of attitude, as sleeker, sassier girls like Anna Wallace might have done. But she had thought at least that there would be some welcome and some guidance for a girl whose head was still reeling from the shock of going from Miss Mouse to nation's sweetheart in the space of a year. And not only did there seem to be no reaching out to her from her husband and his family, but almost – *yes*, a sort of turning away, a turning back to someone who'd been there all along.

She dreamed of Camilla constantly, became sicker and thinner, and it rained and rained. To the Kafka that was her inner life was now added *Jane Eyre*, as she prowled eager and questing through her husband's big cold house, sure she could hear laughter in another room. The laughter she could hear was Camilla's, she was sure – but when she finally flung the door open, there was the mad wife. Herself. She was overjoyed when she discovered she was pregnant; another chance to make a family. But she need not have worried, because help was at hand anyway. And she wouldn't be alone for long, even without her baby.

For during her first year in the public eye, it had been established by editors in the print media that if you put a picture of the Princess of Wales on the cover of your publication, sales would go up by at least twenty per cent. Not only was she about to create a real family; she was also about to come home, albeit to a place she had never lived. She was about to embark on a life in the limelight, whose light would both scorch her and heal her in turn. She had already lost out on love before the ink was dry on her wedding certificate – but just around the corner waited something even better than the real thing.

Getting
Mighty

Crowded

Camilla and her repercussions; the aristocratic institution
of the loveless marriage and the beloved mistress

Chapter 5

Diana

'Camilla'.

As names go, it's a lovely one. Everyone thought so. During the eighties, before we really realized what damage was being done, it was reported that an increasing number of baby girls were being named Camilla, while the name Diana showed no rise in popularity at all. It's easy to see why; it's nowhere near as mellifluous. But the strange thing was that Diana looked like a Camilla – a flower-faced beauty – and Camilla looked like a Diana – a hard-faced huntress.

With Diana about to become 'Diana' in this book, it might be appropriate to examine the third point of the infernal triangle which shaped her entire marriage and in turn made Diana the person she was – the girl from Nowhere who lost a husband and won the world. The classic fairytale story which caught the public imagination so – from rags to riches, or at least from Laura Ashley to Christian Lacroix – was frequently under-scored by Camilla's story, that of the wicked witch–ugly sister who wrecks the life of the beautiful princess. This demonization famously and comically came to a head soon after the revelation of the Camillagate tapes when Mrs Parker-Bowles found herself (in a grotesque parody of the Sloane Ranger habit of throwing things about for fun in restaurants, which the young Camilla Shand had no doubt indulged in herself) pelted with bread rolls in a supermarket near her Wiltshire home by angry women shoppers. (One of the singular triumphs of Diana's appeal is that she was adored even by older, and indeed old, women, not usually a group who fall for a pretty face or put posters on their walls, and would eventually cause even this most Royaltyrespecting group to turn on the ruling house in great numbers.)

At times like this, it did seem that Mrs Parker-Bowles was taking the lion's share of the blame for the prolonged adultery which had so irretrievably devastated Diana. This is easy to put down to sexism and the age-old double standard which makes a sexually active man a stud and a sexually active woman a slut. But blaming the woman who sleeps with a married man more than the man himself can also be seen as a sort of instinctive radical feminist reaction; that men are dogs anyway and women should expect no loyalty from them, whereas between women a certain standard of behaviour towards each other is assumed and expected. The idea of a married man being the property of his wife, whom the other woman 'steals', is also a progressive one. Women fought hard to end polygamy and when we see a woman offering herself as a mistress to a man who already has a wife, we see that woman as a traitor, a sell-out, a sucker-up to men in general. These feelings are perfectly justified and it was simply Mrs Parker-Bowles' hard luck that she was standing by the bread-roll counter that day. She should have known better than to handle merchandise that wasn't hers.

Amazingly, a few very desperate people have tried to paint Camilla Parker-Bowles as some sort of feminist landmark and the one solid touchstone in the midst of a sea of artifice, by pointing out that it was the first time a man prominent in the public eye cheated on his wife with someone older and less beautiful than the wife. This is indeed a tortuous and sorry stab at rewriting history and attempts to imbue it with a dignity it does not have, because when all is said and done it is a story about one woman

Diana

hurting another over a long period of time, without having the soul or imagination to put herself in the other woman's shoes.

It is hard to believe that it is possible to hunt animals regularly for something like thirty years with great enthusiasm – the Morton tapes recall Camilla's persistent questioning of the young Diana on whether she was going to hunt or not – and for it not to have an effect on the character of the hunter. If not strictly a cruel woman, it seems fair to imagine that Camilla is a callous one, with very little sympathy for the underdog (unless he's tearing the throat out of a fox, that is).

To add to the betrayal of Diana, there is, of course, the inconvenient man who squared the triangle; Andrew Parker-Bowles, one of Prince Charles' oldest friends. By the age of thirty-two, Prince Charles had started his second of three long affairs with Camilla (the third of which, started after his own marriage – a boy for you, a girl for me! – goes on to this day), who was by then married. In this episode we can see dramatically how stunted the Prince's senses of duty and responsibility, often touted by his flunkies as his greatest strengths, really are.

We also see how *being royal* can be disastrously bad for your mental health, and that there is more than one way – more than being bulimic and paranoid, say – of being neurotic and psychotic. It is hard to believe that a normal person would consort so openly with a close friend's wife for so long unless the thrill of breaking one of the commandments, of the sheer *droit de seigneur* of 'taking' another man's wife was strong in him. Put simply, Prince Charles behaves as badly as he does because people let him. The first person to say NO to him was, of course, his wife. And for her sins she had to be punished, with her proclaimed the mentally unstable one, albeit that the Parker-Bowles affair does suggest in the Prince of Wales a certain level of emotional autism.

He was miserable because his uncle had died; lots of us are miserable because our uncles die, but we do not automatically respond by jumping into bed with the wife of one of our closest friends. More than that, it was an Army thing and sapping morale something rotten; 'Ma'am,' an old friend of the Queen tells her, according to Sarah Bradford, 'the Prince of Wales is having an affair with the wife of a brother officer and the Regiment doesn't like it.' The Queen apparently looked down and said nothing.

It would be interesting to know if the Prince of Wales, in a private moment, has ever apologized to his friend and brother officer for the humiliation he helped heap on him. It may well be that the Parker-Bowles marriage was what is charmingly known as 'open', but the Charles and Camilla marathon – triathlon? – was conducted over such a long time, involving so many of their friends in providing safe houses and rendezvous, and to an extent so flagrantly (the endless slow-dancing all night at parties which caused more than one Wales girlfriend to bolt) that towards the end Andrew Parker-Bowles was reduced to taking repeated cries of 'Ernest Simpson' at the Turf Club, as well as being charmingly known as 'the man who laid down his wife for his country'. It cannot have helped to have been made 'Silver Stick in Waiting' by the Queen in 1987, whatever her good intentions. *The Carry On*-ness of this title is the final punctuation to the Parker-Bowles sub-plot. While

Diana

Diana's story was a tragedy from beginning to end, albeit a tragedy touched with radiance, Camilla's tale has always been tragi-comic. Any mistress who can reduce a man to dreaming of being her sanitary protection obviously has to have something going for her, horizontally if nowhere else. In another age they could have been happy. But times have changed.

It was all the Queen's fault. Or perhaps it was Queen Mary's, to whom George V when Prince of Wales (and later) was faithful – the first holder of that title to practise such fidelity. Or perhaps it was the Queen Mother's fault, whose husband had single-mindedly worshipped her. But interestingly, neither of those men grew up expecting to become King, and so were allowed to marry for love rather than lineage. It remains a peculiarly sadistic feature of monarchy that while those of the family whose heads do not have to bear the crown are allowed to marry whom they like, and indeed love, those who are faced with the burden of sovereignty generally have not been – an exception is the Queen, who has probably been able to perform her duties so well because she actually married the man she loved despite the disapproval of many at Court. Edward and Mrs Simpson were a low and dishonest pair who, if they had had their merry way, would have had us eating bratwurst for breakfast and saluting a flag which looks like a big ugly spider rather than the red, white and blue beauty which is ours. But when he said what he said about not being able to carry out his job without the help and support of the woman he loved, he pretty much hit the spot.

Prince Charles could have learned from this and married

the woman he loved while he had the chance, in spite of her being boot-faced even at the age of twenty-four and having already been round the block a few times. (By the time of the Dimbleby interview, he had finally cottoned on and made a sort of half-hearted declaration of his need for Camilla by saying that she would 'continue to be a very good friend'. It's hardly giving up your throne for love, but a giant step for a chronic procrastinator like the POW.) But at the time, as in all things, he dithered. Having lost Camilla, he was then, of course, determined to keep her. But something happened. The Prince of Wales no longer found it to be his absolute right to keep a mistress, as Princes of Wales always had, and have his wife and the world turn a blind eye. As I say, I blame the Queen. The wily old bird saw that the surest way of hanging on to her throne was to *appear to be middle class* – plodding around her palaces switching off electric lights and saving pieces of string and, more importantly, making sure people heard about it. What we might despise as miserliness in the man on the Clapham omnibus, we read as down-to-earthness and ordinariness in the woman in the golden coach.

Her dogs and horses and gumboots are another vital arrow in her perfectly aimed bow of banality; and that trick she has, when finally forced to wear the most fantastically elaborate jewels, of wearing them as though they are simply part of a uniform, part of her job, part of the entertainment – an act of drag that is indeed a very real drag for her. There is that inimitable there's-no-fun-in-this-for-me-you-know look which comes over the Queen's face when she is wearing her crown; it may not be glam, but if Marie

Diana

Antoinette had mastered it once in a while and not looked like she was having such a damn good time, the Palace of Versailles might not be empty today, except for the tourists.

The Queen's favourite television programme of all time is by many accounts *The Good Life*, the rather sickeningly twee seventies sit-com in which Felicity Kendall (doing her usual routine as an over-excited eight-year-old boy) and Richard Briers (usual doesn't-know-what-day-it-is routine) turn their backs on their City jobs and attempt to be self-sufficient as small farmers in the stockbroker belt of Surrey. You can see how this must have appealed to the Queen. But by cleverly making her family seem middle class in order not to alienate her subjects, and by stressing that they were very much a family, she made previous behaviour *vis-à-vis* an aristocratic disregard for bourgeois fidelity completely untenable. Remember how shocked people were when Michael Fagan broke into her bedroom and the newspapers revealed that the Queen and Prince Philip didn't sleep in the same bed? Royal experts fell over themselves explaining that amongst the upper classes this was quite common, but to ordinary people it merely established what they had thought for a long time; that the Duke was a bit of a wrong 'un. 'GIVE HER A CUDDLE, PHIL!' the *Sun* advised with lewd concern. By making her family 'ordinary', the Queen kept her head. But when her son lost his and turned once more to Camilla after his marriage turned out not to be to his liking, he found himself on very shaky ground. For who could believe in *A Good Life* in which Tom was habitually unfaithful to Barbara with Margot?

It had all been so different once upon a time. Given even less chance to marry for love than other people, the monarchy has always felt much less compulsion to be faithful. In Henry VIII, the most enthusiastic serial monogamist of all, we see this at its most sensational, but other kings merely left their wives on the side of the plate for Mr Manners when they tired of them, rather than inside a bucket. The glory and spirituality of monarchy, the divine right of kings and all that blasphemous mumbo-jumbo about the monarch being His representative on Earth seems even more profane when placed alongside the prolonged delight with which monarchs have broken their marriage vows.

The type of prim and proper citizen who sees the monarchy as a totem of purity in a dirty world should have no truck whatsoever with history books lest he find himself reading about 1324, when King Edward II had a retreat built on the south bank of the Thames, staffed and stuffed with whores for his relaxation and recreation. Or 1431, when Henry VI visited France, and was entertained by three naked women frolicking in a fountain – he was ten at the time. (And we think it's a little bit racy for Prince Harry to get an eyeful of all those topless African dancing girls!)

And of course 1660, when Charles II returned to the throne of England, bringing with him a huge influx of aristocrats determined to resume the lifestyle which Cromwell had so rudely interrupted. Being a leisured class and, additionally, one highly pleased with itself for returning from the routing handed out by the New Model Army (which sounds like a good enough description of Prince Andrew's girlfriends before he had the good luck to hook up with Miss Sarah Ferguson), one of the

Diana

main functions – and indeed the only talent – of the aristocracy was to be seen enjoying itself, and no King was ever as suited to this onerous task as Charles II, whose courtesans and mistresses took up easily as much of his time as did affairs of state. His friend the Earl of Rochester wrote the following about him:

Peace is his aim, his gentleness is such,
And love he loves, for he loves fucking much.
Nor are his high desires above his strength;
His sceptre and his prick are of a length. . .
Restless he rolls about from whore to whore,
A merry monarch, scandalous and poor.

Which does make you wonder, recalling the saccharine suck-ups of John Betjeman and Ted Hughes, why we can't have Poet Laureates like that anymore. Can you imagine what the Earl of Rochester might have done with the Tampax tapes?

Barbara de Villiers, Frances Stewart, Louise de Keroualle and the charming guttersnipe 'Mistress Nelly' Gwyn; these were the principal mistresses of Charles II, interspersed with a never-ending stream of the pick of the capital's whores and actresses. At the time of the Restoration, London resembled one big brothel to the extent that any courtier, City financier or politician without a mistress became a figure of fun. So much for the idea of revolutionary governments promoting free-for-all street orgies while reactionary ones promote family life!

The Restoration period so degraded marriage and revered sexual incontinence that Catherine Sedley, born in 1657 the only heir to a large fortune, chose to become a courtesan rather than to marry because that way she could hold on to her own money and indeed increase it while enjoying a freedom and independence far beyond that of a respectable, disrespected aristocrat's wife. Not blessed with the temporary visa of beauty but rather the permanent passport of charm and wit, she became mistress to the King's brother, the Duke of York, after being placed at Court as maid of honour to his wife. When the Duke became James II she was rewarded with a yearly pension of £4000, created Countess of Dorchester and Baroness Darlington. When James II was ousted by the Protestant William of Orange, the new king so respected Miss Sedley that he gave her a pension of £1500 a year; still only thirty-eight, she married a soldier and lived grandly off her inheritance plus all the jewels, riches and titles she had gathered as a royal courtesan until the age of sixty when, still happily married and independently rich, she died.

It was the exact opposite of the Dating Do's And Don'ts that Barbara Cartland always preached; then, if you were a young girl who saved your virginity for your husband, he was likely to think you a fool, not to mention a bad bedmate, and leave you at home to rot while he caroused with low-born whores. Even discretion was a complete unknown during the Restoration period; aristocratic men found playmates at public houses and at brothels patronized mostly by the common people. Catherine Sedley's own father (obviously the original Lad) was brought to trial (while fearing no punishment from his peers on the Bench greater than a few weeks banishment from Court, all the better to dry out at his country home in readiness for the next inevitable pub-crawl) for becoming drunk at a public house, coming naked onto the balcony above the street, miming all forms of sexual congress known to man or beast and parodying the scriptures in a downright filthy sermon before taking a glass of wine, washing his penis in it and drinking the King's health! This, in broad daylight, in front of a thousand people! They don't show you that on the lid of the Quality Street tin.

It was hardly surprising that Catherine Sedley rejected the mandatory early marriage with such an example of husbandly behaviour before her very eyes; lewd times or not, married women of the aristocracy were permitted no such licence. And the hypocrisy of the times stunk as badly as the sewers; Samuel Pepys recorded that the King 'usually came from his mistress's lodgings to church, even on sacrament days; held as it were a court in them, and all his ministers made applications to them'.

Just as men have always sexually abused women and adults always sexually abused children, the working class was always sexually abused by the ruling class. But as the eighteenth century progressed – though progressed is hardly the word – there came to be an element of almost genocidal sadism about this casual contempt. In London, the Mohocks – gangs of young male aristocrats – terrorized the people of London by night, raping and murdering women for kicks in a manner far pre-dating *A Clockwork Orange*. Their parents formed societies such as the Hellfire Club, kidnapping and raping young working-class virgins, particularly in the ruins of churches. In France the Marquis de Sade specialized in the torture, imprisonment and poisoning to death of working-class women.

It was not, despite all the Restoration romps, a time of great sexual liberation but rather of great sexual oppression, as the women who took part in such bacchanals were largely uncon-senting and working class. There was a real hatred in the sexual conduct of the aristocracy of this time, which must partly stem from the fact that they were still smarting from the humiliations the Puritans had quite rightly heaped upon them for being so utterly sleazy and unworthy of their power. Now, once more, the rich would get the pleasure and the poor would get the blame. Not to mention the clap.

But the poor did not take it lying down all of the time. Young working-class men, in particular, were so mortified by the fact that their sisters and mothers were whoring for the rich that they habitually threatened royal mistresses in their coaches, while in 1688 a group of apprentices smashed up the Moorfield brothels, one of them later saying before his hanging that they did 'ill in contenting themselves with pulling down the little brothels and did not go to pull down the big one in Whitehall'.

By the time that James followed Charles, he was shrewd enough to house Catherine Sedley well away from Whitehall and to issue instructions that no courtier be drunk in front of the Queen, Mary of Modena, who repented each day to her Italian confessor for the rouge she felt forced to wear by the fashionable women of the Court. The wind of change was blowing through Gropecunt Lane (an actual street name in the London of the time), and with the deposing of James II and the crowning of the upright William of Orange, who turned his back on the Court to rule from Hampton Court rather than Whitehall (which was burned down in 1698), it blew that particular house of cards down. It may be that William and Mary had gone in search of their own *Good Life*; whatever the case, the days of the royal *dolce vita* were gone for good.

Just as the British monarchy embourgeoised itself in order to live (contrary to popular experience, in which one must reject the bourgeois state in order to live fully), the royal paramour underwent a similar process. By the time of Edward VII, they were no longer whores, foreign aristocrats, orange sellers or other such loose cannons, though actresses remain popular to this day – think of Susan George and Koo Stark, who with the artifice typical of their breed have managed to display complete discretion.

Lily Langtry was a prototype of the new bourgeois mistress as patronized by the then Prince of Wales, but the epitome must have been the Honourable Mrs George Keppel. In her case, the 'Mrs' was a far more attractive part of her title than the 'Honourable', meaning as it did that she would be very unlikely to become possessive or otherwise cause trouble. During the courtship of the Prince and Princess of Wales, according to Andrew Morton, she asked him about his previous girlfriends and he had told her with complete shamelessness that he preferred married women because they were 'safe'. It seems frankly shocking that the man who plans to become head of the Church of England should apparently see marriage not as a sacrament but as a talent pool which makes a woman worthy of receiving a royal rogering; perhaps the

Prince's devotion to Islam and his preference for being Defender Of Faiths, rather than *the* Faith, stems from his desire to have more than one wife – regardless of whose she is.

Mrs Keppel was the soul of propriety; on the day of the Abdication, she was dining at the Ritz and was heard to say 'Things were done so much better in my day'. She slept with the King at least three times a week, went on holiday with him twice a year on the royal train and advised him on presents for his wife. To add insult to injury, she kept a large signed photograph of the King's wife, the beautiful and fragile young Danish princess Alexandra, prominently displayed. Her great-granddaughter Camilla Parker-Bowles would appear to have been a veritable Estella to her Miss Havisham, though with a burning contempt for women rather than men.

And contemptuous such behaviour was, despite the cosy witterings of the King about his 'Dear Mrs George' – contemptuous and quite hideously hypocritical. Such behaviour made it perfectly clear that, while the proles waved flags and cheered themselves hoarse, events of allegedly national importance and spiritual relevance such as royal marriages and Coronation vows were rituals that must be endured, but which essentially meant nothing to the men who made them, at least. Princess Alexandra, half-deaf and unable to walk properly, would probably not have chosen to have herself delivered in such a vulnerable condition to a man who had no intention of loving her, had she had a choice. Though knowing the state of morals of the merry monarchs of Windsor, a wife who was hard of hearing probably counted as a plus.

Diana

Mrs Keppel, meanwhile, was cut from the same coarse cloth as her great-granddaughter; she considered a vulgar hat worn at the races far more shocking than mere adultery. His ministers all approved; Sir Charles Hardinge wrote of the 'excellent influence' she had over the King, who true to form, looked at his Kennel Book, ate too much, drank too much and smoked too much but was, nevertheless, easily bored and the proud owner of a vile temper. Mrs Keppel, who once said that her job was 'to curtsy and jump into bed', kept him amused for twelve years by changing her clothes four times a day and throwing wildly expensive parties for him. To help foot the fantastic bills, the King found Mr Keppel a lucrative job as a buyer for Liptons and introduced Mrs Keppel to his banker Sir Ernest Cassel, who literally made a small fortune for both her and the King. So cosy; and to poor foreign Alexandra, barely speaking the language, hardly hearing a thing, about as cosy as a nest of vipers.

They look well together and each looks as good as they ever will

There is a photograph from the early part of the seventies (a period which often seems to have had more than its fair share of shimmering, sunlit Indian summers to those who grew up in it; see the current early seventies nostalgia for what seemed like a time of unsurpassed freedom, post-Pill and pre-AIDS) of the Prince of Wales and Camilla Shand, as she was, standing together by a tree, seemingly unobserved, in profile. He has been playing polo; they are casually dressed and rumpled, and utterly blind to everyone but each other. They do not seem aware that the photograph is being taken at all, though the camera seems close and we only see them from about the waist up. It brings to mind the scene in *West Side Story* when the star-crossed lovers first meet at the dance in the gym, and around them all the room and people fade away, leaving only their rapt faces in clear-cut close-up.

They look well together and each looks as good as they ever will. He has not yet lost his hair, nor she her lips. Between them there is a tree, on which a heart has been carved, and inside that heart there is a 'C'. It is the most beautiful picture of Prince Charles and the woman he loved ever taken; not the engagement pictures which went on all the mugs for the mugs, not the Kiss, not those posed *Country Life* jobs *en famille* for the Christmas cards.

We hear so much about the bravery, the progressiveness and the fearless quest for change which burns inside the Prince of Wales like the heartburn from Hell. Then why could he not, on this most important of all issues, marry a woman of his own age with a modest amount of sexual experience, knowing that she would in all probability make him happy for the rest of his days? Why did he drag a third party in, an innocent third party who would go to her early grave irretrievably damaged by such a monumental sting? What in the world possessed him not just to blight the life of the woman he loved, but of the woman who loved him? One thing is sure – on that day in the Mall, in front of those jubilant millions, we saw who did it: Judas, on the balcony, with a kiss.

Where
do yc
my lc

u go to,
vely?

Diana of the sorrows and her failing marriage

Chapter 6

Diana

She was the same as us in a lot of ways, and that's why we liked her so much and straightaway. But in one way she was very different, and that was why we loved her, always and forever. It was what made her such an old soul yet such an insecure one. She had seen it all, but she never stopped flinching.

It was this: whereas most of us get a chance to *settle down* at some point in our lives, Diana was only ever *shaken up*. Her normal childhood was shaken up by her parents' very public divorce; her teenage home life by the coming of Raine; and her schooldays by her repeated failure to achieve. For a few brief months she finally found it in her London flat, watching *Crossroads* and wondering at the exoticism of the banal. How knowing and worldly the waitress Diane, queen of the cold trolley, must have seemed to Diana, with her bottle blonde hair, orange sunbed tan and abrupt advice to those less road-tested than herself: 'Abortion's not a dirty word, you know!' And vampy Sharon, the garage owner, with her married men and Chianti lamps, and backward Benny with his white mice and premonitions. All the mysterious splendour, in fact, that was King's Oak on that treacherous cusp when the slippery seventies gave way to the excess of the eighties.

But suddenly all that was over before she was even out of her teens, when one middle-aged prince made a bad, sad decision, and one naive nineteen-year-old woke up to find that the world was not so much her oyster, more her albatross and her catwalk. 'Growing up in public' is a phrase which has become immensely popular with people who have spent any amount of time, however small, in the public eye or indeed even in the pop charts, peaking for one week at number thirty-four just before Christmas some time in the seventies while in their early twenties. Its use usually signals a personality so full of itself and so fancying itself that it just might conceivably get itself pregnant if left unsupervised in the same room as a mirror for any amount of time.

I never heard of Diana using the phrase; no doubt she considered that all her growing up had been done behind closed doors, where her heart took the shards that would change its rhythm forever, from the absence of Frances to the presence of Camilla. But it suited her more than any other individual I can think of; from virgin to wife to mother to megastar, all in the space of three years. To give an example, Madonna left home at nineteen and made it at twenty-five; that took six years of solid pushing by somebody who desperately wanted fame. Diana had half the time and twice the fame; to say that it cannot have been easy for her to adjust to the many-mawed mob suddenly screaming for her, in addition to marriage and motherhood, is to take English understatement into the realms of the surreal.

Anyone who had a heart would have helped her; told her that they were a team, that it was a bit like ballroom dancing, and that all she had to do was follow his lead until she picked up the rhythm and spun happily into the solo spotlight. Not Prince Charles. He was too busy.

However hard you try not to, there are times when anyone reading about the life of the Prince of Wales will be forced to lay down their book, sigh deeply and think 'Exactly what is that guy's problem? It's hardly going down a mine for a twelve-hour shift each and every day, now is it?' There is an old popular song which goes 'I'm busy doing nothing/Working the whole day through/Trying to find lots of things not to do/I'm busy going nowhere/Isn't it just a crime/I'd like to be unhappy BUT!/I never do have the time.' All of this would seem to apply to the Prince of Wales except the last line; being unhappy, striding the Balmoral moors with angst in his pants, sitting at the feet of merry old Sir Laurens and getting himself into even more of a state, seemed to be something he could always find time for as a newly married man. So was endless polo in summer and hunting in winter, in addition to the ten weeks official holiday he takes each year and generally spends fishing and painting. 'If I didn't get the exercise, or have something to take my mind off things, I would go potty,' he once said, displaying the sense of duty and love of his role we all know so well.

But one wonders what 'things' are. The Prince of Wales often gave the impression in the eighties that the strain of his position was all too much for him, as the previous statement implies. But then you had to put this next to his avowed desire and eagerness to be King. Surely he was aware that the business of being the actual monarch was a damn sight more stressful than merely waiting to be the monarch? And that actually doing more work, not less, might be the solution to his problem of just waiting about for his mother to die?

But Prince Charles is notorious for losing interest in the many projects that flit through his transom in the course of a working year, even if ten weeks of that year are devoted solely to royal R'n'R. He has, for a long time, been the despair of his many advisors who, with all the appalled yet ever optimistic anticipation of the wife of a serial philanderer, watch as he moves through the inevitable Five Boys-type cycle of discovery, enthusiasm, start-up, cool-off, abandonment. And incredibly, by the January of 1982, less than a year after that wedding and with his wife three months pregnant, Project Diana seemed to be just the latest whim with which the Prince was quickly tiring.

The combination of chronic morning sickness lasting all day, the pressures of being looked at all the time and the continued suspicion that her husband was once again involved with Camilla combined to provoke in Diana, in that first year of marriage, behaviour more often seen in the so-called Muppet Wing of Holloway Women's Prison than in the royal palaces of Britain. These were the actions of the lonely starlets who haunted Hollywood Babylon rather than those of a thornless rose from the misty heart of England; the self-destructive behaviour, and most spectacularly of all, throwing herself down the staircase at Sandringham to land at the feet of the horrified Queen, who summoned the royal gynaecologist from London. It obviously did not occur to the Queen to summon her eldest son instead, whose determination to go out riding rather than give his wife some attention had sparked the incident in the first place.

It was certainly a far cry from the home life of our own dear Queen. Her early married life had been reportedly the happiest time of her life, before the trials of ruling took over. As a young wife on a naval base in Malta she played house with a man she was obviously mad about – and who, for all his later short-tempered appearance of suffering from the worst bout of dyspepsia ever known to man, did seem very keen on her. Looking at the photographs of Prince Philip and Princess Elizabeth on honeymoon – there is one especially where they are just walking along laughing into each other's faces, taken at the unfortunately named Broadlands – it is clear that, at the risk of sounding both coy and lewd, he made her feel like a woman and she made him feel like a man. The Prince and Princess of Wales were obviously not as lucky; he made her feel like mutilating herself and she made him feel like going out riding.

the Queen was having some sordid sixties social realist melodrama being played out right before her eyes

To give her credit, the Queen must have been absolutely amazed. In the world she came from, young women did not throw themselves down staircases and slash at themselves with lemon slicers. *That* was the behaviour of – if not the jungle, then at least the working-class council estate! *Cathy Come Home...Poor Cow...Up The Junction*; the Queen was having some sordid sixties social realist melodrama played out right before her eyes, right under the portrait of Papa, God rest him! For a woman whose upper lip was stiffer than her mother's preprandial G&T, such behaviour must have seemed literally incomprehensible. For the Queen, like many of her class, had only ever seen male anger; female anger, so inward-looking and self-destructive, must have seemed very much like madness.

As a woman who found it notoriously difficult to show her feelings to anyone who could get around on less than four legs, it would be unrealistic and presumptive to have expected the Queen to sit Diana down and offer her a massage and some TLC. But what the Queen might have managed was a word in her eldest son's considerable ear. But, as with the affair with Mrs Parker-Bowles that so displeased the regiment, she saw no evil, heard no evil and spoke no evil. And this is all it takes to allow evil – or, in this case, brute callousness – to flourish handsomely.

Considering Diana's almost fanatical love of children, how unhappy must she have been to have risked her baby's life by throwing herself down a flight of stairs and all the other things? She must really have felt like a prisoner by now, the 'Prisoner of Wales' she would later talk about. And like *The Prisoner*, she had been removed to an alien enviroment in which everyone knew what was going on but her, and where it seemed she was being punished for something she didn't understand. She was a prisoner as surely as the baby she was carrying, but for her there was no warmth and oblivion. Just the darkness; this was the start of what she would later call 'the Dark Ages'.

111

Diana

Project Diana sewn up and the heir implanted ready to hatch, the proud putative father saw fit to return to his old role as son rather than husband, often provoking screaming rows with his wife as he yet again left her to go to his mother. This would worsen with the arrival of the children, when he was heard to say on two separate occasions 'I love William and Harry dearly, but sometimes I just have to get away from home to get some peace' (of his tendency to lunch with his grandmother at Clarence House) and 'I've discovered I don't like four-year-olds' (of his eldest son's behaviour). Growing up, he had always been the centre of attention as the heir to the throne; suddenly, people were more interested in his children than in him.

For a man with very little to recommend him in the way of natural talent, accomplishment or intellect, commanding attention had become in itself the *raison d'être* of his life. Perhaps for this reason, he seemed to find it hard to take the natural pride that anyone else would in his wife and children; for if they were beautiful and beloved by the public, surely that took away some of the finite amount of public affection there was for him. It's a fair point; by 1991, Diana had finally overtaken even the Queen in popularity, let alone the ageing Prince. Perhaps there really is only so much blind peasant devotion to the English ruling classes to go round. (For some reason Prince Charles seems far too old to be a prince, whereas Princess Anne does not seem too old to be a princess. Perhaps this is because she has character and can carry off any title. It is easy to imagine her as a Dowager Princess, whereas if Prince Charles is still a prince in ten years' time, he will be a laughing stock.)

But long before the children were born, he was jealous of Diana. The meek little mouse who had seemed happy to stand in his shadow, or indeed on a lower step in order to make him look a bigger man, woke up one day and roared. In the beginning, though, she seemed to be shining up a treat; fearful, fragile and thinner by the minute, every shrinking inch just the sort of malleable Plasticine princess from which a third-rate man could draw infinite comfort from *vis-à-vis* his superiority. Diana, it appeared, had gone from loving comfort food to being comfort food: his.

Arriving in Wales in the October of 1981 for her first major engagement since the wedding, people saw Diana shivering in the rain, two months pregnant yet almost two stones lighter than the nursery school Madonna with the Betty Grable legs backlit by her last summer of freedom. Yet in sickness, as in health, the people loved her; for the first time, it was a contest and there could be only one winner. A more enlightened man, especially a self-made man, could have managed this with a small amount of rueful humour; one can easily imagine the raised eyebrow and bumbling charm of Denis Thatcher, say, at the start of the reign of Queen Mag. But for Prince Charles it is clearly another thing to feel resultful about.

She was what they wanted – but there wasn't that much of her, not back then. The blonde beacon, striding out like a great white goddess gleefully accepting the tributes of a triumphant nation, was yet to come; for now she was a slip of a girl – from Supersloane to Superwaif in one short misalliance – doing her

113

best to put her best foot forward and accept the hands and bouquets without crushing one and dropping the other. Yet even then, when the crowd's attitude to her was more one of protection and affection than adoration, there were the first signs of it. *'Diana....Diana...'* – that rather plain and brittle name moving like a Mexican wave through the crowds, their Welsh voices giving it the sound that 'Maria' had for Tony in *West Side Story*. Say it loud and there's music playing – say it soft, and it's almost like praying.

She used her clothes as a drag and a camouflage

She wore the Welsh colours, green and red; the people liked this little courtesy. It was the first time clothes came to her aid, speaking for her when she felt too frightened to speak for herself, and through the years her inarticulate speech of the heart would often come out in this way. One has grown so used to the silly chatter of rag hags, all of them without a truly modern, original or sophisticated thought in their heads but insisting that everything you put on should 'make a statement about who you are' and in the end one thinks warmly of the Fran Liebowitz quote: 'If people don't want to hear from you, what in the hell makes you think they want to hear from your clothes?' But with Diana it was different. She used her clothes as drag and a camouflage, and when she finally found her tongue she gave away her gowns to charity. When this Empress had no clothes, it was because she no longer needed them. As some clever Frenchman said, the truth loves to go naked.

But in the wintery Wales of 1981, her self-respect almost subterranean, Diana needed all the help she could get from her clothes. Except gloves. She was always weird, but good-weird not bad-weird, about gloves. Her friend Anna Harvey of *Vogue*, the first fashion mentor credited with getting her out of Laura Ashley's death-by-sprigs once and for all, wrote in 1997: 'She made a conscious decision to dispense with formality very early on. I ordered dozens and dozens of suede gloves in every shade for her because the Royal Family always wore gloves. Heaven knows where they all went because she never wore any of them. She wanted flesh to flesh contact.' That was it, you see; from the very first public flesh-pressing, she had always seemed the only member of the Firm ever to seem actually happier among *the* people than with those who were supposed to be *her* people.

Over the years, the legions of Windsor-lickers in the media – and there have been many once-high names on this roll-call of shame, goodness knows! – have tried to construct various 'unconventional' personas for the members of the tribe. Prince Philip: speaks his mind, whatever the consequences! Princess Anne: down to earth and doesn't suffer fools gladly! Prince Edward: royal rebel who rejected the demands of the army for the roar of the greasepaint and the smell of the crowd! Princess Margaret: Bohemian diva, who knew that living well was the best revenge! All well and good. But nine times out of ten here,

Diana

'rebel' equals 'rude, especially to the public'; and you couldn't believe for a nanosecond that any of them would rather be out in the streets meeting the people than holed up together playing charades in words of less than one syllable. Whatever their differences, they were still one unit, bound together by their distrust of outsiders.

Not Diana. From the start, her public smiles of elation and tears of compassion were a stark contrast to the look of sheer boredom and dread which could so easily cloud her face during gatherings of the clan. Later on, when her public life was in full swing, she only ever skived off on the supposedly precious family leisure time, forever fleeing Sandringham and Balmoral and hopping on to a public-service plane in order to get back to London and DO something. And the gloves were the first outward sign of where her loyalties lay; in our hands. Interestingly, she did often wear them on family occasions, when she might have to touch them; this was no phobia, but a cool, insolent choice.

How much of a choice was her bulimia? Whatever one says about bulimics one risks offending them, and they are notoriously touchy people due to all those hormone levels plunging and vitamins evacuating the building three times a day. If you say that bulimics choose to do what they do to themselves, then you fall into the hands of the snap-out-of-it lobby. If you say that they have no choice you take away the one thing they feel they have any control over. I think it is fair to say that after the first few exploratory excavations – vomiting, like heroin, takes quite a few goes to get addicted to – the body is in such a state of nourishment deprivation that, as with someone who has not had enough sleep for several weeks, the very act of choosing is not what it once was. Therefore a bulimic may choose bulimia, but on the other hand may have found the two options so lacking in any real difference – the difference between being murdered or committing suicide, say – that snapping out of it seems neither here nor there. All they know is that they feel worthless, that people do not want them, and so it would be best if they just disappeared. But! – and here the bloody-minded human spirit raises its head, the one which differentiates the bolshy bulimic from the apathetic anorexic – they'll do it *in their own time, thankyouverymuch!*

She could control her weight, then, and, as it turned out, she could control herself. This girl who would only ever appear in school plays if she could have a non-speaking part, and who spent much of that first time in Wales in transit tears, begging her husband not to make her face the crowds again, had a miraculous way of pulling herself together when duty called for it – so much so that for years her obvious 'happiness' with her new life poured scorn on anyone who said otherwise, even herself. Pregnant, sick, new to the job, one can contrast this with the oft-displayed nastiness of those 'born to it' – Member Of Public To Princess Anne: 'It's a shame it's been raining.' Princess Anne: 'It's stopped now, so what are you moaning about?' Member Of Media To Prince Philip: 'How was your flight, Your Royal Highness?' Prince Philip: 'Have you ever flown? Well, that's what it was like.' – and conclude that while blood may well be thicker than water, no one is thicker than a Windsor in a strop.

Diana

Like in the old song, she made us – if not Them – love her. And perhaps this is where the long mutual love affair with the people began, because it was the first love she had seen in a long time. She could touch it, even, for this love had a thousand hands, all reaching out to her, and she could see it in a thousand eyes, all shining it at her. 'The people who stood outside for hours and hours, five or six hours in torrential rain, that's what I remember,' she was to say many years later. 'They were so welcoming. Because I was terrified. But they made it much easier for me.' She made her first ever speech at the end of the 400-mile tour and attempted a few words in Welsh. Speech was already her second language anyway, a long way after touch; foreign tongues held no more fear than her mother-tongue did. She might as well just do it.

The singer Janis Joplin once defined the great problem of fame as 'making love to five thousand people onstage and then going home alone'. This syndrome, the lonely-at-the-top routine, tends to mistake effect for cause; i.e. if Janis Joplin, Marilyn Monroe or any one of the secular saints hadn't been famous, they'd have been happy. Whereas it is pretty obvious to anyone but the sickliest sentimentalist that Janis, Marilyn and all would have been just as miserable if they'd made teenage marriages to meat-packers and spent their days in mobile homes in Montana. Fame was the bodyguard which kept that ultimate stalker, sorrow, at arm's length for a while; it was never the stalker itself.

What makes a star is not that *little something extra* but rather that *little something missing*. And Diana was missing a lot; freedom, love, her health, her youth. But the camera loved her, even in her diminished state, as did the microphone. In fact, her sickness and fear somehow became weapons in her armoury, making her deliver speeches, like the one she made at her first solo public engagement of turning on the Christmas lights in Regent Street, in a rapid monotone. She sounded shy and, somehow, not quite posh – the glottal stops, the mumbling – which, for a restless people increasingly impatient with what appeared to be a cold, uncaring monarchy, made her quite perfect because she didn't sound like one of Them. Had she been confident and healthy, she would have done, and love would not have come quite so quickly.

But something changed. They say that we become our masks, and no one ever became their mask as beautifully as Diana. There is an old Jewish saying: in the end, it is easier to call your mother than not to call your mother. The day we realize this, confidence comes; the day we realize this, that shyness is hard and confidence is easy, is the day the adolescent becomes the adult and the amateur becomes the professional. It comes at different times for all of us but when it does it's like having an electric lightbulb switched on in your soul; it shines out of your eyes and warms you up, all the way from inside. And soon people are holding out their hands to you to warm them. For you are the fire, the fire and the phoenix both.

And this baptism was about to drop, like a mercury tear, onto Diana, Princess of Wales, turning her at last from a girl into a woman, a goddess and, finally, a legend.

Reach
Out a

nd Touch

Diana finds happiness in her work for the common good

Chapter **7**

Diana

'When the heart breaks open/So much you can't hide/Put on a little make-up, make-up/Make sure they get your good side, good side.'

By 1983, when she undertook her six-week tour of Australia and New Zealand and was mobbed as few women since the fifties screen queens ever have been, she was Adam Ant's 'Goody Two-Shoes'. And like Goody Two-Shoes, shod by Rayne, she was the very model of a modern, moderate young woman. 'You don't drink/Don't smoke/What do you do?' What she did was bulimia, which was by now a sort of discipline in those lost years after normality and before the workout.

You can see how bulimics justify their habits for weeks, months, years. You can see why they even manage to convince themselves that they're being good. The slimming industry, which all through the Keep Fit and banting crazes of the early part of the century was seen as a bit of harmless fun, has become a multi-million-pound industry and a matter of life and death. The rise of the sedentary lifestyle, which has affected the rise in weight gain throughout the whole population, has seen a shrill, nasty scrutiny on the part of the modern media, especially the tabloid newspapers, of the increasing weight of women in particular.

Even in the habitual mega-million meat-markets of entertainment, men do not face the same pressures to look perfect. The rules are so different for men – Woody Allen's wizenedness, Dustin Hoffman's dwarfism – are routinely reinterpreted as 'off-beat' sexiness. Men alter perceptions to accommodate their bad features; women alter themselves. It's as big a difference as the one between self-defence and suicide. Nowhere is this truer than of body mass. Gross Jack Nicholson, pudgy Harrison Ford, positively huge Robbie Coltrane; there is not one man so obese that he cannot somehow be accepted as a sex symbol. The female celebrity, however, is hounded with the zeal of McCarthyite witchhunters on the trail of a particularly premature anti-Fascist, particularly by English middle-market tabloids such as the *Daily Mail* and *Daily Express*. In these papers – uptight, misogynistic and absolutely terrified that some woman somewhere might be having a good time – we see amazing feats of double-think when it comes to the body image of women. One day female celebrities such as Judy Finnigan or Baby Spice will be castigated for daring to wear bikinis on bodies which err on the 'wrong' side of robustness; the next day a tragic pair of twins who starved themselves to death will be featured, fully made-up and looking like concentration camp survivors in a grotesque parody of fragile femininity. That anorexic girls start off on the road to starvation because women are judged on how rigidly they can control their weight, and because of the same morbid fear of female flesh, never seems to occur to these overgrown playground bullies.

The more famous a man, the fatter he is expected to get, to demonstrate his wealth and the fact that the rules about health and efficiency no longer apply to him. But the more famous a woman gets, the thinner she must get. In Bruce Willis and Demi Moore we see the perfect illustration of this. They started

Diana

out a pair of moderately attractive, medium-sized people. Now he looks like Homer Simpson, and she looks like Barbie Doll. It is amazing to us to recall that while Marilyn Monroe was an American size sixteen dress, Jennifer Aniston is an American size four. In fact if Marilyn was around today, it is unlikely that she would be given romantic leads, or even be considered sexy by the Hollywood studios. Rather, she would get the Rosie O'Donnell parts; pretty, skinny Meg Ryan's best friend whose idea of a hot date is a cup of drinking chocolate with marshmallows on top. It is as though the better and bigger women become in the real world, the less space they must take up to make up for it.

And no sooner was Diana Spencer at last given some attention than – ever the good girl, obedient pupil and dutiful daughter – she started to fade away. Only the fact that she was pregnant stopped her from disappearing, and even then at times she looked like a thin cartoon animal who had swallowed a cannonball, as thin cartoon animals are wont to do. The tabloid photographs of her in the Bahamas, five months pregnant in a bikini, were obscene in more ways than one; she literally looked like an incubator, built to humanoid approximations.

Her bulimia threw into even starker relief the exact reason why she had been drafted into that Family; to produce an heir. At one point, all the nourishment she took in must have been going to the baby, for Prince William when he was born on 21 June 1982 was a strapping creature, blond and bulky and pleasingly unlike a Windsor except for the fact that he whined a lot of the time.

If ever any woman was not physically or psychologically ready for the underwater dread of postnatal depression, it was Diana. But the straw that broke the camel's back also helped it go through the eye of the needle, or at least into the eye of the hurricane. She must, one day, just have looked in the mirror after a session of bulimia, or postnatal weeping, or morning sickness, or crying over Camilla, or any combination of them, and said: 'Right, Diana Spencer! Best foot forward!' She would later claim that she got the gift of putting on a brave face from her mother, a lonely legacy, but more use than anything else her parents had given her. When she finally realized that all was lost – that is, her husband to another woman, and her dreams of a happy marriage to dust – she finally saw when that dust cleared that there was nothing there at all and that she would have to build it all from scratch.

Very early on, she began planning her life effectively as a single parent. And after the initial shock, as many women in the real world find, it was actually easier to deal with one demanding child without a husband than deal with two demanding children, one of whom is a husband. Before long, things were looking better than they had in a long time; her son gave her something to live for and her bulimia gave her some control.

And coming up on the outside, there were a couple of other things. She was about to become the biggest fashion icon the twentieth century had yet seen, and that would be why we never stopped looking at her until it was too late. But more than that, she was about to reach out and try to help anyone

Diana

who had ever felt as sad as she did. And that was why we never stopped loving her. As far apart as they seemed on paper, the two things always went hand in glove. Albeit that the hand was not waving but drowning and the glove would never be worn as she took the hand of the dying yet again.

According to Andrew Morton, it took Diana six long years before she got used to being looked at – and towards the end, when the paparazzi's hounding of her as a single woman became as sexual as stalking, it was a gift which deserted her and must have, as much as his big brown eyes and gentleness, attracted her to the security blanket of the al Fayed boy. But she seemed happy to be looked at much earlier on; she didn't know, after all, that one day she would be looked at to death. She seemed happy as soon as she got her clothes sorted out, like most women. Many sad rich women seek consolation in clothes, but Diana's shopping was something different, and at times almost an addiction, though one which actually worked, helping her through the worst times until the time came when she no longer needed them. Everyone has crutches; it's just that most crutches don't cost £3000 and come from Versace.

At first, Diana wore her clothes not so that people would look at her, but because she hoped they wouldn't see her. And if her disguise was good enough, everyone would be too busy oohing and ahhing over the new Conran or Hachi or Azagury to notice her and realize that it was just 'Thicky' Spencer playing dress-up. Simone de Beauvoir famously said that 'One is not born a woman, one becomes one,' and in the same way that a drag queen hides his howling pain under the ritualized shield of hairdo, makeup and gown, so famous and fragile women hide their panic under a bushel of bravado. She quickly learned that she could rely on clothes, not people, to give her confidence. Still, it is sobering to think that as she went out and did her best each day as a young wife, her tights were giving her more support than her husband was.

She had come into the public gaze with little more than the clothes she stood up in, and they (bless them) – that blue engagement suit which made her look like an air hostess! That frilly blouse! That wretched jumper with the sheep on it, like an insomniac's nightmare! – were proof indeed that only cats are born with style; humans have to learn it. Diana recalled in the Morton tapes that she had as a private citizen owned one long dress, one silk shirt and one pair of good shoes; even when she and her mother went out and bought six of everything, they were told by the Palace that it just wouldn't do. What was needed, it explained, was four changes of clothes each day from January to December. And this from a House that boasted about saving tax-payer's money by saving string! Couldn't they have used the string to make her a couple of bikinis, at least?

Both of Diana's sisters had worked at *Vogue*, and in 1980 *Vogue* journalist Anna Harvey was asked by the editor if she would like to help Diana Spencer, just engaged, put her clothes rail together. In the October 1997 issue of *Vogue*, Miss Harvey wrote with simplicity and elegance of the experience, starting with the first time they met. 'Her eyes lit up when she saw all

Diana

the racks – I don't think she had any idea how many lovely things there were out there.' You would have to have been a saint to be a newly slimmed-down, five foot ten girl of nineteen who had grown up thinking FUS culottes the height of fashion and not gone a little mad, like a kid in a candy store.

Miss Harvey pointed out that Diana knew nothing about fashion, like all girls from her background – 'There were no It girls then.' Diana, she wrote, 'wanted to be modern rather than fashionable,' to the chagrin of the rag hags who obviously wanted her to go the whole hog and make herself look as insecure, obsessive and sad as they, with their endless search for novelty and their ceaseless ability to make fools of themselves. But the true fans of pure fashion are the people no one would ever pay to sashay down a catwalk or to make love to a camera; the designers and fashion editors (hardly ever even Paint-by-Numbers let alone oil paintings when it comes to looks). They have a vested interest in watching a pretty girl being taken down a peg or two in front of the world's press wearing a beekeeper's outfit complete with muslin mask, a T-shirt saying SLUT or shackles on her wrists and ankles. Fashion, which was once about gilding the lily, has become ugliness's revenge on beauty.

Diana knew this, and leaned towards the conventional in dress, as all true rebels do. And another reason that she wasn't really high fashion is that she was low fashion; she had a common streak a mile wide for which the glossy posse often mocked her before she became the patron saint of their beloved AIDS charities. She loved – at different times – blond streaks, blue eyeshadow, white stilettos, sailor collars, one-shouldered 'Dynasty' dresses, polka dots, ankle socks, costume jewellery, kohl, cowboy boots, baseball caps, knicker-bockers, fishnets and (sss!) Virgin sweatshirts.

She knew what she liked; to look like one of the common people on her days off and to look like a professional when performing. That she saw her clothes as costumes first and foremost reflected her cavalier attitude to fashion, that greedy and gormless god. She had too much of a sense of humour to be really fashionable and she was too down-to-earth. The couturier Roland Klein once arrived at his showroom to find Diana, who had turned up early, helping his assistant wash up – catch Naomi Campbell doing that! And, typically, she paid for all her dresses promptly, unlike many a royal female free-loader, whose tardiness in paying up has made them the scourge of London couturiers.

With Anna Harvey, Diana would study newspaper photographs of every public occasion to see which outfits 'worked' and which did not; the act not of a narcissist, but of a professional determined to do her best with a very poor hand. Over the years the Designer Di tag began to upset her and she turned away from glitz and to Catherine Walker, who defined the up-and-at-'em pizzazz of her later life.

From very early on – the tears not yet dry on her pillow, as Dame Barbara might have said – being up-and-at-'em was how she saved her own life. For a woman in the grips of bulimia and emotional torment, unloved by her husband, racked by morning sickness and by homesickness for a

Diana

simpler life, the sheer *Out Thereness* of Diana's early public life was amazing. The Queen became convinced that Diana was a problem when, during her first pregnancy, she would force herself to attend public engagements and then quite understandably be on less than sparkling form. The Windsors thought it better form to cancel. But then, the Windsors are not the Spencers.

I'm Dancing As Fast As I Can was the title of a book by an American ballerina spinning out of control on her addictions to drugs and bulimia, but it describes well the world of the young Princess of Wales, the momentum of whose fame seemed to build to an hypnotic-compulsive tempo recalling the fairytale *The Red Shoes*. She had to keep moving because she feared what she might see if she slowed down. But unlike the restlessness of most of the rich and the ruling class, hers was no mindless jetsetting search for distraction in order to take her mind off the emptiness of her life, but a real desire to make things better, for them and for herself. And that was why Diana was never seen as a Lady Bountiful figure, one of her great fears at first; very soon, the people who came to see her or the people she saw in hospitals and hospices, realized that she needed them as much as they needed her – more, in fact.

Despite (because of?) her own problems, she had, within a couple of years, established herself as a fresh, unpretentious breath of roll-up-your-sleeves, the-show-must-go-on, best-foot-forward Englishness amidst the Gothic Glamis-Graeco-German gloom of our very own dysfunctional First Family, our own little House of Usher. She had a knack for making

duty look like fun. She seemed excited when she saw the size
of the crowds and luminous with sorrow when she held the
hand of a dying man. She seemed thrilled when she received
bouquets, and often looked at small children as though she
frankly wanted to kiss them all over, in the nicest possible way.
After decades of seeing boredom writ large across those loveless Windsor mugs (the delight Diana took in a crowd of
people, the Queen has only ever been photographed showing
when she looks at a four-legged friend) whenever they were
called upon to meet their people, it was no wonder we fell for
her so heavily and so quickly.

In factories and schools, unveiling plaques, planting trees
and shaking hands, launching ships and tying shoelaces, on
her knees to play with children and on her best behaviour with
foreign dignitaries, home and away, she was soon averaging
five public engagements a week, more than any members of
the Royal Family except the Queen, the Duke of Edinburgh
and the Prince of Wales. But it was the way she did them. A
member of the public coming away from an encounter with
one of the other royals would typically feel mildly dismayed,
as though they had made some unspecified gaffe and embarrassed the Great One, who had remained noticeably stilted
and ill at ease throughout the brief exchange. They weren't to
know that the Royal Family speak to all 'outsiders' (though
looked at logically, both racially and numerically, it is they
who are the deviations) this way. Even the Queen Mother, who
because of her common hats and Cockney teeth has always
been seen more as 'one of us' than the others, relies on that old

Diana

chestnut 'Aren't the flowers wonderful?' when mingling with the hoi polloi.

Diana, in contrast, looked as though she literally couldn't get enough of people, whether tenderly holding an old lady's face in her hands, staring soulfully into the eyes of a man with AIDS or lifting a twelve-year-old boy with cerebral palsy right off his feet with the swooping strength of her embrace. Little things meant a lot when she did them; she could say silly little things which were so profoundly sweet because she said them solely to put people at their ease. 'I've got a mouse in my muff', she once remarked to a shy little girl, not realizing the *double entendre* therein. 'My bottom's black and blue', she told a startled old man after sitting on a wicker chair, perhaps with flirtatiousness beyond the call of duty. 'Thick as two short planks, me', she told a jobless teenager. 'No sense, no feeling', when she bumped her head going through a low doorway. It was not Martin Luther King, but it was a way of saying far more than the words actually spoken. To a woman in the crowd who waited six hours in the driving rain to see her first set foot in Wales: 'Poor you! I feel cold myself – you must feel much worse. Thank you for waiting for us.' *Poor you.* It is literally impossible to imagine any other employee of the Firm putting themselves in the shoes of the little man for sixty seconds at a time, let alone thank them for waiting. That it took so little courtesy from a royal to send her straight to the top of the popularity polls showed how fed up the British people had been for those years without even knowing it. Thick as two short planks she may arguably have been back then, on the dotted line at least, but just as we showed Diana what she could be, she showed us what we could have.

The clothes were an important part of this new way of being royal. Other royal women dressed in the dull pastel uniforms of Norman Hartnell, with sensible shoes and stuffy hats, their shortness and pear-shape adding to the illusion of one of those irritating dolls with the leaded bases that won't lie down however much you shove them. This bespoke not a devotion to duty overriding all frivolity particularly, but rather the smug conviction that there was absolutely no need for them to ever make an effort.

But by making herself a spectacle as well as a crusader, Diana smartly avoided being tarred with the Lady Bountiful tag she so feared. When she put on her gladrags and got out there, there were distinct overtones of the professional performer who, for all that, still loves the sound of the crowd. She made such an obvious effort with the way she looked that it came across to the crowds as a kind of compliment to them; as someone once said of a pop group, 'Their music is applause for the audience.' As her hairdresser Sam McKnight told *Vogue*: 'She was always concerned with being appropriately dressed, whether it was for a factory opening or a première. She never wanted to make people feel uncomfortable. She always wanted to please. Sometimes I'd say to her "Your hair looks fine" and she'd reply "But Sam, these people are expecting Princess Diana. They'll be disappointed if they see me looking dowdy".'

Diana

Sometimes she seemed to do so much that the phrase 'Hasn't she got a home to go to?' came to mind. Well, she had a nice big house and sons she adored more than anything on earth. But a house is not a home, and sons are not a husband.

When the Prince and Princess of Wales finally separated, when the tired and tattered bunting was finally taken down, he asked her to make a list of everything she wished to take with her to Kensington Palace from Highgrove, the home always destined for him and Camilla. She had married a prince and gone all around the world just to return a bachelor girl again, to a lush SW apartment. Only this time it would be much lusher and much lonelier, and *Crossroads* was long gone, as long ago and far away as her girlhood.

At the top of the list she wrote 'Paul Burrell'. Paul Burrell was a young man from the shut-down pit village of Grassmoor in Derbyshire, the son and brother of miners. He first met Diana at Balmoral when he was twenty-two and she was nineteen and not yet engaged to the Prince of Wales. She was lost and he showed her the way. He never stopped and she was to refer to him as 'my rock' when, as her butler, he was to be the one constant presence in her ever-shifting life. When she died, only he from outside her immediate family was allowed to take the boat across the lake at Althorp and watch her being laid to rest.

It was Paul Burrell who, more than anyone, persuaded Diana that her reaching out to people like those he had grown up with – the people of England, and Scotland, and Wales, and Northern Ireland, who had never spoken yet – would be met not with scorn and ridicule, as she feared, but with sheer, spontaneous delight. And it was in his cottage at Highgrove, watching her sons play with the Burrell boys and befriending his wife Maria (who had been Prince Philip's maid: not a job description most young women would feel up to, I think), that she might have realized that not everyone was going to treat her the way that people from her own class always had; with condescension, callousness and cruelty. As a friend of hers told her confidante Richard Kay of the *Daily Mail*: 'Paul always used the word "humble" when he talked about his background, but to Diana he and Maria represented the best things in life; decency and honesty in what she saw as a sea of deceit.' It was a poignant turnabout of the Lady Chatterley myth; the aristocratic woman who sought out the working-class man so that he could teach her about integrity and fidelity as opposed to the carnality and sexual incontinence of her own kind.

'It was the warmth she wanted,' Richard Kay's source said. 'She found herself learning about a life and hardships she had never known.' And like an up-close-and-personal version of her public life, she always approached the Burrell family not as a *grande dame* but as a lonely young woman, eager to learn all she could. The Royal Family may have treated servants 'well' in their time – the Queen and Prince Andrew are supposed to be particularly polite – but they never became friends with them before. Yet when we see the two other boys with William and Harry in snapshots from Thorpe Park

Diana

and Disneyland, those are not, as we always thought, school-friends from Eton but rather Nicholas and Alexander Burrell, the grandsons of a miner, their adored companions. When her sons were away from her after the separation, as they were a great deal of the time, it was the Burrell boys she begged to come to Kensington Palace to play with the princes' toys and destroy the sad silence of absence that was now her companion.

Paul Burrell was with her in hospitals and hospices, in Angola and Bosnia, in sickness and in health, for better or worse. After she had been stripped of her title, it was he who, though in service to the Windsors since the age of eighteen, never failed to address her as Your Royal Highness. Turning down offers of work from everyone from the Queen to Tom Cruise and Donald Trump (and we can imagine with teeth-grinding embarrassment the swanking and gloating that would go on over having acquired 'Diana's butler', and that's just at Balmoral), Paul Burrell has refused to countenance another job until his present task, an inventory of all her possessions, is complete. Working through the twenty rooms of her apartments, from the abandoned nursery once used by the princes to the private drawing room where she sat, abandoned, speaking into a tape recorder and trusting a man she had never met to tell the truth for her, Paul Burrell must walk like an eagle-eyed Orpheus in the Underworld, making lists and tidying up after a Persephone who will never follow him away.

'A tear is an intellectual thing,' said William Blake, and in Diana this somewhat baffling phrase was made flesh. Diana cried not out of sentiment, but from a profound and intelligent vision of another world, one which was taking such a long time coming. She was a true Utopian, the exact opposite of both her husband with his mumbling and promising and 'Something-must-be-done'-isms and her husband's family with their morbid belief in continuity above all else.

Diana's reaching out was, as yet without tongue, a random and reflexive thing. But just a little more hurt, another sharp turn of the screw and she would find her words and her way home; transformed not by love, but by pain.

Broken

Wings

The making of the finished Diana; stronger on the breaks

Chapter 8

Diana

Despite the fact that Diana's flesh has not yet fallen away from her bones, rendering her yet another of the vast grinning army of ivory soldiers, an army in which Greta Garbo and Mao Tse-tung could pass for twins, it somehow does not feel indecent to write about her. And there must be two reasons for this: one, that mankind is a shameless animal who can convince himself of anything when there is a wolf at the door and a living to be made; and two, that Diana's relationship with the media was to some extent a Morganatic marriage; a uniting of desires never allowed into the throne room yet which sustained both parties long after the ritual of royal romance had grown rancid.

It does not seem impolite to write about her love affairs and her bulimia, her sorrow and her joy, because she showed us these things, volunteered them as exhibits A and B and beyond, trusted us to take them as gospel and pass the word on. But it does somehow feel wrong to write about her love for her boys. For this was, of course, the only thing that ever went right for her, and therefore seems so foreign to us.

No one has a problem with the idea of motherhood; motherhood and apple pie have become synonymous in their banality, even, when evoking the American Way. But the reality has gone so stale that even papers which habitually whip themselves into a frenzy over the sanctity of family values automatically take potshots at any passing mother should the opportunity arise. Underage mothers, overage mothers, single mothers, lesbian mothers, surrogate mothers, working mothers, state-supported mothers. And, of course, every rapist,

murderer and TV licence-dodger has one thing in common –
they all had MOTHERS! Case closed! No wonder the birth rate
is plummeting; mothers just can't win. Diana knew this.
Initially recruited to give the Windsors an heir, she did so well
that in the end it became yet another stick to beat her with; that
she was too wrapped up in them, too friendly with them,
forever dressing them up in baseball caps and trainers in order
to feed them burgers in homeless hostels and theme parks.

Mrs Parker-Bowles has been a good wife to the man she loved, if not to her husband

There was nothing that Diana excelled in so much as being
a mother. She made it look brave and bold and new. Neither
the simpering angel of the hearth who devotes her days to
finger-painting and breast-feeding nor the neurotic career
drone with three nannies, she made having children seem as
exciting and essential a part of life as crusading for good or
going on holiday. But in her very triumph of innovation, she
highlighted a problem that faces many modern women; that
being a 'good' wife and being a good mother are hardly ever
compatible, despite the bleatings of the Family Values (that
famous hypermarket!) lobby.

Diana

The Queen was a good wife; everything her husband wanted (except changing the name of the Royal House to Mountbatten) he got. She was such a good wife that rather than rock the boat she let her husband construct educations and careers and eventually marriages for his children which would lead to nothing but heartbreak. She was such a 'good' wife that standing up for her children's interests against her husband was beyond her.

Mrs Parker-Bowles has been a good wife to the man she loved, if not to her husband. One of the things which has reportedly kept Prince Charles so tightly bound to her down the decades has been her complete and total willingness to fit in with whatever schedule he has planned. One of the most poignant aspects of the Camillagate tapes were the amazingly complicated and tortuous arrangements which the lovers made to meet each other at the 'safe' houses of their friends for a blissful night of sin. Involving her intricately detailed knowledge of the West Country motorway system and his encyclopaedic roster of her children's school holidays and her husband's brief visits, they plotted like seasoned campaigners planning a drop in enemy territory to snatch a stolen hour, drawing in many of their friends who were in on the affair both as alibis and landlords. That many of these friends were not just aware of the relationship but positively getting in there with their sleeves rolled up to make it work, must have depressed and humiliated Diana even more than the silly, smutty sex talk.

'I'd sacrifice anything for you. That's love. That's the power of love,' says Camilla at one point, and we utterly believe her;

husband, children, marriage, anything. For this dog-like devotion she is rewarded with the head-turning tribute from her paramour: 'Your great achievement is to love me.' And at first it sounds like a terrible insult, but of course it's true; Camilla Parker-Bowles has spent her entire life on horseback, tormenting beautiful creatures, or on *her* back, tormenting one particular beautiful creature. And apart from that, she has had no life. What more could an old-fashioned guy like the Prince of Wales want?

Too late; he had picked himself a spirited, high-stepping beauty, and he was saddled with her. All he could do was make himself scarce whenever possible; this ironically seeming to strengthen, not weaken, the family unit of Diana and the boys. He always looked wrong, even in the photographs that had taken ages to pose, even in the Christmas cards.

She clung to them with a love that looked like amazement. No public children have ever been so royally loved. Think of her in that red and white check suit, arms flung wide as she seems to fly towards them on board the *Britannia* after a short separation or in a blue and white frock with William in a Wimbledon box, almost seeming to swoon as she looks down at him. She had been taken on as a brood mare, then an animal she would be; fiercely devoted to her offspring and increasingly indifferent to the male, who having impregnated her for nothing more than some old biological drive, felt free to wander as he chose.

Being told by the Queen to leave Diana alone, we gentlemen of the press pretended deference but soon caught ourselves smirking down our sleeves; 'Why? So you can have her all to yourself, so nobody can hear her scream?' When the Chairman of the Press Complaints Commission condemned the press for 'dabbling their fingers in the stuff of other people's souls' after the publication of the first Morton book, we knew him as possibly the only person on the planet who hadn't caught on that the book was Diana's own message in a bottle. When her brother condemned the press at her funeral, we wondered why he had worked as a journalist specializing in society tittle-tattle. No, only one rebuke rings loud and clear and ever will: that one word, MUMMY, on a plain card on the white flowers which her sons placed on her coffin. It is a cry from the heart and from the abandoned nursery for a good mother who wanted a little fun, just a little, stepping into a car beneath the night sky of Paris, gone forever. She is the Lost Mother, mother to all the Lost Boys but most of all to her own. And that card speaks of a loss far greater than any of us will ever know. Because even though she pretended sometimes, because she knew it made us happy, she never belonged to us – the People's Princess! – at all. She was theirs and only theirs.

And they were only hers, very soon. According to the Morton tapes: 'As soon as Harry was born it just went bang, our marriage, the whole thing went down the drain. I knew Harry was going to be a boy because I saw on the scan. Charles always wanted a girl. He wanted two children and he wanted a girl. Harry arrived, Harry had red hair, Harry was a boy. First comment was "Oh God, it's a boy", second comment "and he's even got red hair". Something inside me closed off. By then I knew he had gone back to his lady but somehow we'd managed to have Harry.'

For a people supposedly so in tune with the natural world, for whom hatching, matching and dispatching are not the stuff of drama but the rhythm of life itself, as inevitable as the seasons, what a source of endless pain, disappointment and cruelty the begetting of children seems to be for the ruling class. Whether it is Earl Spencer sending his wife on a round of ritual humiliation in Harley Street, Charles Windsor carping that his wife has not managed to come up with the standard pink and blue 2.4 fittings and fixtures or Charles Spencer putting his sick wife through the rigours of childbirth four times in four years in order to secure an heir, and actually going so far as to admit to his mistress in a letter that he had brought innocent children – the three girls – into a marriage that was wrong from the start just so he could get that heir, they actually seem to have less feeling for the facts of life and the joy of sex than the most careworn teenage single multiple mother trapped in a tower block in Tower Hamlets. You have to ask again, why don't they just marry women they love? 'Because there are two types of women; mistresses and wives' the old answer would have been. But more often than not in the twentieth century, male aristocrats marry the glamorous, fragile women – Frances, Diana, Victoria – and have good-humoured, healthy carthorses for their mistresses. Surely it was meant to be the other way around?

Whatever; in late 1982, a blazing row between the Prince and Princess ended with him telling her that his father, the

Diana

ever-enlightened Duke, had told him that after five years of marriage he could go back to his old ways; for example sleeping with any married woman he cared to other than his wife. The lines were drawn, the gauntlet was down and the gloves were off.

Now see Diana run; faster and faster, Princess Toadstool unbound, as she entered the third and most dangerous level yet of this incredible world she had found for herself. As in some fantastic video game, this blushing kindergarten girl had fallen through the blocks and found a whole magical hidden place; life as the first ever Royal Pop Icon. For only her face of all of them can you imagine Warholized in bright primary colours, the sad blonde brazened into life by the flat dimensions of fame.

At her first level she was Princess as Pop Fan, calling up Capital Radio to wish DJs happy birthday, queueing at McDonald's, screaming on the water chutes at theme parks. Then came the Princess as Pop Star, copied, screamed at, smiling from magazines. She met celebrities as one of them, at least to their eyes, and they were often unbelievably coarse. 'We shall get you a part in *Dynasty* when you come to Los Angeles,' oiled Joan Collins. 'She's beautiful – tall, blonde, just my type!' leered the unspeakable Rod Stewart after meeting the Princess in one of the eternal pop line-ups for the Prince's Trust.

But just as this was becoming mortifying in the extreme, a new Diana emerged from the lurex and lip gloss: Princess as

Pop Svengali. Perfectly catching the zeitgeist, she suddenly became more serious – almost statesmanlike. Her speeches, coached by Richard Attenborough, began irretrievably to drive the pompous pontifications of her husband not just from the front pages, but the news pages too. And with an ease that made every alleged media Machiavelli from Madonna to McLaren seem positively inept, this shattered marionette picked herself up, dusted herself down and started pulling the strings.

They say that each new decade actually begins in the middle, and the eighties only really began for most of us in 1985, just as the nineties only began after Mrs Thatcher left office. By 1985, her reproduction duties complete and her husband back up to his old tricks, Diana decided to concentrate on three things; her boys, her charity work and the business of being the beloved of what sometimes seemed like the whole world. Motherhood, sainthood and sex idolhood – you couldn't really blame the press's eyes for popping out on stalks and never going back in again.

In the years between 1985 and 1992, a love affair took place between the world's media and one woman, of the kind that made everything that had gone before look like amateur night in Dixie. Marilyn Monroe and Jackie Kennedy look, in retrospect, like Ugly Sisters doing their best to stand in for the blonde tornado while she was learning how to walk, how to fall and how to get on her feet again (for the first time out of many) in her nursery in Norfolk. Considering these women and the kind of global fame they both enjoyed and endured, it

Diana

is pleasing to realize that Diana comes across as far more of a
Marilyn – warm, witty, self-made – than a Jackie, despite the
fact that socially she had far more in common with Mrs
Kennedy, who will surely go down in history as the most
elegant doormat who ever lived.

But for a member of the British Royal Family to party up
such a storm with the guys wearing green eyeshades and
pencils behind their ears! 'It was a blonde,' an American
reporter murmured, quoting Raymond Chandler, as the affi-
anced Diana oozed out of the car in That Dress, her breasts
clearing the way for her ten minutes ahead. 'A blonde to make
a bishop kick a hole in a stained-glass window.' True,
monarchs had died for the press before; the fatally ill King
George V on 20 January 1936, his hour brought forward by his
physician with an injection of cocaine and morphine at 11.55
pm so that he might die before midnight and have his death
reported in the morning *Times* rather than the *déclassé* afternoon tabloids. But no one had ever loved the press before.
Diana loved them up a treat and they did her proud.

Every famous person has a press office, but at one point,
the press was Diana's press office. Like the Lowells and the
Cabots in New England, they talked only to each other, it
sometimes seemed. After the initial post-honeymoon tantrums
and tears – before she realized that her anger should be
directed at the man who would take her life rather than at the
men who would take her picture – she soon settled into a
mutually supportive relationship with the media which
seemed to give her far more pleasure than her marriage had

ever done. In his great book *The Queen*, the historian Ben Pimlott pinpoints the moment when it was made clear exactly whose foot was in whose door:

> One clip of film taken early in the marriage illustrates well the contrast between Diana and her in-laws. It shows a royal group entering a room for a formal banquet. While the Windsors glide in with eyes straight ahead, Diana pauses for an instant to pat her hair and give the waiting cameraman a half-flirtatious, half-apologetic 'We're all in this together' look. The style – that of an actress or a politician – transformed royalty from dignified-but-dowdy into fashionable.

Fashionable, the monarchy fashionable! Never such days! For it remains a paradox of British life that while still ruled on the hereditary principle, what is popularly if naffly known as 'street style' is developed in this country, and has been since the 1950s, to an extent unknown in the more democratic France or United States where most young people simply want to look richer than they are. But here, it is cheap and cheerful working-class youth, from the Teddy Boys to the Spice Girls, who have decreed what that season's Look will be; even the most exclusive and expensive of British couturiers such as John Galliano and Vivienne Westwood attempt to identify themselves with 'street' fashion while producing ornate monstrosities that few ordinary people would dare wear in the street for fear of being

Diana

lynched. 'The young working class dress so much better than the young middle and upper classes,' the designer Katharine Hamnet once said to me. 'The reason the young working class dress so well', I couldn't help but tell her, 'is because they can't afford your clothes.'

It was the frocks which drew them at first, a swirling kaleidoscope of colour which soon saw even the most spit-and-sawdust of the old Fleet Street snappers learning the difference between a Conran and a Lacroix. But it was the way she looked at them rather than the way she looked that held them. When the elderly *Sun* photographer Arthur Edwards complained that she had worn what she was wearing before, she bounced back 'Arthur, I suppose you'd prefer it if I turned up naked.' 'Well, at least I could get a picture of you on the front page that way,' he answered. When Mr Edwards fell ill, she visited him with medication; in Egypt, she threw a party for him. On one occasion she amazed a group of royal reporters by asking them if they remembered what a large bosom she had had as a teenager.

Her preference seemed always to be for the tabloids, in complete contradiction of King George's product-led death. 'You're from the *Financial Times*? We took that at home,' she said to one preening hack. 'Yes, I believe we used to line the budgie's cage with it.' At first she played the media like a kitten on the keyboards; she was skittish, no-sex-I'm-British, flirtatious and gawky, like a colt not yet inclined to bolt. She was so *ENGLISH* and how very sexy that word is, long before the EC surveys found that we had it more often than everyone but the Danes. *Innn* – the dark deep interior – *glishhh* – the lush glide to a lip-smacking finish. But with time the kitten disappeared and Diana and the press began to play each other like a beautiful four-handed piano duet, as instinctively in touch as the Labecque sisters at their best. Or like a brilliant, solitary figure skater, she looked down into the ice and saw her reflection, and it had many heads and they all carried cameras around their necks.

She was their creature from the beginning and with them she conspired to win even more power. 'Oh, you should have seen those Arabs going ga-ga when they saw me on the Gulf Tour,' the journalist Judy Wade once heard her swank to her press posse. 'I gave them the full treatment, and they were just falling over themselves. I just turned it on and mopped them up.' But there is, of course, a chance that she actually felt sorry for the gentlemen of the press as much as anything else and was simply trying her best to make their jobs easier and their lives more bearable. We all know how Diana loved a lame duck and male journalists are a generally unprepossessing and dysfunctional bunch, more prone than many other men to drinking and divorce and every sort of city sorrow. How strange it would be if when Diana was pursued by the press when she went to visit the needy, she saw no difference on either side of her; just a lot of people who needed her to look them in the eye and heal their lives, some of whom got paid for it.

It wasn't enough.

She was patron of one hundred and twenty charities, and

Diana

it wasn't enough. Encouraging young people to stay off drugs, women to demand the sort of childbirth they wanted, homeless hostel-dwellers to swear off the demon drink. It wasn't enough.

Since 1985 Diana had had her act consummately together, glamour and goodness firing from both hips, but the level of attention she commanded was not equal to what she was giving back. Unique among the Royal Family, Diana always understood that towards the end of the twentieth century, respect cannot be demanded but has to be earned. As does a living; she wanted to give the people who paid for her beautiful dresses something for their money. Everyone was looking, and she had to give them something big to look at or merely atrophy into just another swank society beauty strutting between fundraiser and charity ball.

And in the end, she found the thing that her dresses would eventually go to raise money for, hostages to her new streamlined life. She found the big disease with the little name: AIDS. These were the years of Deep Charity, as in Deep War. And she chose a place in which to stake her claim as a crusader, not as a clothes horse, not weeping, where all was dark and dread, the shadowy side of the street where no Lady Bountiful had yet dared tread. *Here Be Dragonnes.*

When it came to good works – well, the Windsors would rather go and kill something, frankly. But when forced to put a metaphorical penny in the poor box, the cans they rattled or at least gave their name to bore the likenesses of lifeboats, nonhuntable animals such as pandas and old buildings; things that could never answer back, didn't need to be talked to or even dream of committing an embarrassing gaffe or familiarity. Even battered children were that bit too controversial; the RSPCA is Royal, but the NSPCC is merely National, though with their track record, the Firm had a bit of a nerve putting their stamp on the first one, let alone the second.

To show what a go-ahead ball of fire he was, positively straining at the leash to embrace the dispossessed of the world, Prince Charles had taken to joshing with jobless teenagers and cheery Rastafarians in the seventies. But there was a limit. Long before AIDS, when Diana was reaching out to the disabled, the deaf, the blind, the elderly and the homeless, her husband was already sneering at her 'Diana The Martyr'. And this from the man who one day hopes to have these people as his subjects! Well, she might as well be hung for a sheep as a lamb, and a black sheep at that.

In the eighties, it struck me that there were quite a number of interesting parallels between Diana and Madonna, then the two most visible women in the world. Both were motherless children from boring backwaters. Both were voluptuous brunettes who became skinny blondes. Both were regular little party animals, saying no to drink, drugs and smoking and exercising like things possessed. Both had big noses; both were good dancers; both married extremely ugly men. Both were wise virgins, losing it only as a 'career move' as the bolder of the sorority put it. And both were the only real first-rate celebrity crusaders against AIDS, a cause now justifiably associated with the shallowest sort of showbusiness addlepate who sincerely believes that all they have to do is put on a pair of clear-glass spectacles and a red ribbon to join the ranks of the great and the good.

In the past, Diana's world tours had been primarily things of beauty; it did the battered and bruised humiliated English heart good to see her queening it over the rebellious Australians, their republicanism mysteriously mutated into a million paper Union Flags, or knocking out the eyes of skeletal society mavens in Washington as she danced with John Travolta and trashed once and for all any sort of sniggering over the allegedly dowdy dress sense of the modern Englishwoman. This time it was different. She started off in London, opening the AIDS unit at the Middlesex Hospital where, incredible as it now seems, not just the attendant press but the patients themselves were amazed when she shook their hands without wearing gloves, as was her wont. Why were they amazed, after all that time? Didn't they know what she was like, what she needed by then?

'It meant more to me than anything,' one of the men said later, while in a few years' time a prominent London AIDS doctor would say 'A handshake from her is worth a hundred thousand words from us.' That AIDS was incurable must surely have contributed to the almost mystical descriptions of Diana's power at this point – 'Can't do them any harm, can it? And if it makes them happy. . .' – but it remained a real possibility that to these men, to whom glamour had always been the Holy Grail, the sight of her all done up like a glossy magazine dream may well have sent their immune systems rocketing. In 1989 it was a former AIDS nurse himself, now suffering from the disease, who said 'She is doing as much for AIDS sufferers as any doctor or nurse.'

In 1988 she went alone to New York, where she visited seven dying children in the AIDS ward of the paediatric unit at Harlem Hospital. The staff cried as she cuddled, talked to and played with the children, who were all black. The director of the hospital, Dr Margaret Heagarty, described Diana as 'a deeply sensitive and kind young woman. Our own royalty, whatever that is in a republic, have not done anything nearly so symbolic as these things you are doing for us today. Your presence here and your work in Britain has calmed many people.' In a country as rabidly bigoted as the United States, where no child with AIDS was allowed to be photographed for newspapers, lest as already had happened, their homes would be burned to the ground, calm was what was needed before anything else could possibly be achieved.

In 1990 she revisited Washington DC, where she went to Grandma's House, a children's home for AIDS victims. One dying three-year-old girl, nicknamed 'First Lady' asked her 'Can I ride in your car?' 'Of course you can,' answered Diana, picking her up and carrying her out to the British Embassy Rolls-Royce, and there sitting her upon her lap to ride through the city. 'The Princess is a wonderful person, and she really does care,' said the Reverend Debbie Tate, president of the orphanage.

Grandma's House, 'First Lady'. . .the whole shebang of America's monumental sentiment, while whole American

Diana

families were giving each other AIDS by sharing needles and American presidents would never in a million years have driven a child dying of AIDS through the nation's capital in a state car for fear of what it might do to their majority in the Bible Belt. In such situations it was very clear why Diana was as appealing to Americans sick of their presidents as to Britishers sick of their monarchs. Because she didn't care, by this time, what people thought of her. She just cared.

And what was her prince among men doing all this time? He, who cared so much about humanity, who allegedly never wavered when it came to going out on a limb, against the grain, embracing something new? Well, he called her visiting of the AIDS babies in New York 'totally unnecessary', according to Kitty Kelley, and when photographs were understandably published of her hugging a dying black baby this veritable Titan of integrity found them 'predictable'. He found his wife's interest in AIDS in general 'inappropriate' and 'sentimental' and gave credence to such reports when in Brazil in 1991 he preferred to plant Brazilian nut trees – culminating with a friendly pat and a 'there you go', greatly pleasing the country's journalists who knew them as 'Cinderella And The Man Who Talks To Plants' – while at an AIDS hospital in São Paolo Diana hugged and kissed deserted, dying children, presented thousands of pounds' worth of medical equipment to AIDS research laboratories and talked through a translator to adults with the disease. Crying, she later said, 'The things I have seen here are beyond belief. 'Back in Britain, she collapsed with dengue fever, a local disease.

Prince Charles, ever the sleeves-up, hands-on mucker-in abroad, ended his Brazilian trip by chairing an ecology seminar aboard *Britannia*, moored thoughtfully near the mouth of the Amazon but forever an air-conditioned little piece of England where a fellow could avail himself of clean water and, of course, ship-to-shore telephone lines to his mistress.

Four hours after getting off the plane in England, he was playing polo. Whatever else that man Wales was, he was certainly a man with his priorities right. A few weeks later he would demonstrate his Olympian sense of perspective once more when his son Prince William was lying in the Great Ormond Street Hospital For Sick Children having been rushed there in an ambulance after sustaining a fractured skull. How could the neurotic keenings of his wife compare to the thrill of *Tosca*? After being informed by doctors that a CT scan had found a fractured skull which needed surgery straight away, Prince Charles left them both, the unconscious boy and the too-conscious woman, to go to the opera, where no doubt he cried, as he often does at music. A sensitive man; a lover of beauty; a lost cause.

A sensitive man; a lover of beauty; a lost cause

Diana

This was, even as she shone and stroked and kissed her way through the AIDS hospitals of the world, the beginning of the end. These were the opening bars of the final, refined version of the Diana whose death would cause the half-Mexican, half-medieval oceanic outpouring of grief we witnessed that terrible day in the autumn of 1997. This was the perfection and redemption of Diana which would find its final expression, its final resting place in the image of the beautiful, serene woman in the crisp white shirts and the old khaki chinos, the sun in her hair and murder in her eyes, standing there between two maimed children and just daring some politician to say that landmines could somehow be justified. In seeking to defend life, her life would now largely be about death.

Chronicle Of A Death Foretold: it is all too tempting to claim with hindsight that Diana's early death was likely or even inevitable. But it is true that she lived her life with the self-conscious speed that those destined for an early death tend to. A virgin until the age of twenty, a secular saint by the age of thirty-six, she packed an immense amount of living into her sixteen years as a woman. In the last few years of her life, although she looked more lovely and as youthful as ever, there already seemed to be something of the winding down about her mortal coil; her boys were off her hands, taken away by school, divorce and the ever-reaching tentacles of the House of Windsor, her retreat from public life was underway and her second marriage was about to be settled. The ever-increasing dependency on spiritualists and clairvoyants seemed something more appropriate to a woman much older.

She realized she was empty, so she became a vessel. She realized everyone was looking, so she became a camera. She was broken by now – her husband, his mother and his mistress had seen to that, thank you – but she was better, in both senses of the word. She was not as natural and spontaneous as she had been before, but as F. Scott Fitzgerald documented of himself in *The Crack-Up*, she was actually stronger at the break. She would need that strength more than ever now.

Only the
L

onely

Divorce and media downfall

Chapter **9**

Diana

Opinion is divided on when exactly the marriage of the century (or rather the marriage of nineteenth-century hypocrisy to twentieth-century candour) came to an end. Was it on the honeymoon where the bartered bridegroom carried his mistress's likeness in his diary? Was it in Korea, where their dismay and distraction at the mere thought of even having to sit next to each other transformed the usual banal round of Ruritanian receptions into an alienated Scandinavian melodrama on the fine art of marital combat? Was it ever truly alive to start with? How many mistresses can dance on the head of a pin?

Diana, Princess of Wales, who was probably better placed than all of us to say when, told the Friends of Morton that her marriage ended the day Prince Harry was born in 1984; once her husband had literally got what he wanted, which was not in this case sex, but the heir and the spare, as the upper classes so sensitively put it. (What a great start to a child's life, to know that he is the 'spare'.) It's funny; when working- and middle-class girls are warned by their mothers that a man only wants one thing, it means sex. But with the uppers, it means a male baby.

By 1991, their tenth wedding anniversary, rumours of the marriage's death would have been impossible to exaggerate. And the nineties were to herald a half-decade of anguish and anomie for Diana before her final triumphant curtain call – loser and still champ! – of 1996, when she finally scraped the House of Windsor off her shoes, and which would last until her death.

The eighties, despite the demonization of Margaret Thatcher by the misogynistic liberal media, was a good decade for women. From the miners' wives who coped with the devastation of their villages by discovering a new wealth of strength and aspiration within themselves, to the power-dressed girls of various hue and heritage whose only interest in ethnicity was the 'city' bit, the eighties – built as they were on effort and merit rather than the old school tie – welcomed women as no peacetime decade had before. Then, they had been making munitions; now they were making waves.

The Diana who finally fought her way through sickness and deceit and cruelty and who came out the other side like a soldier emerging from a treacherous tropical jungle swamp looked like the eighties; streamlined and strong, built to fight and win. A conspiracy between genetics and gym, Harvey Nichols and health club, diet and designers, she epitomized the healthy body clothed by a healthy credit card (the healthy mind could be put on hold, to attend to once the desk was cleared) that was the eighties idea. Diana, after her Prim Period (dressed in frills) and her Pizzazz Period (dress to thrill), took to power-dressing like a halibut to H20, forever striding towards the camera on her way to shake hands with yet another charity director in skyscraper heels and short-skirted, bright-coloured suits, and you could see why. She had been powerless for so long that even dressing the part must have felt like a step in the right direction.

Power-dressing was frequently derided – mostly by men who were bad at their jobs but had managed through a

Diana

combination of low cunning and high connections to hold on to them through the seventies and who in the eighties woke up with a start to discover that the gawky girl from the typing pool was coming up on the fast track. (A bit like Prince Charles.) The Yuppie woman became in the eighties what the witches had been to Salem: convenient Aunt Sallies for everything that men most disliked about themselves, be it lust, greed or the ability to drink three bottles of Chardonnay straight down after work and then roll home to tell the spouse that they'd been working late.

When media men welcomed the 'softer, caring nineties', they were merely expressing the hope for softer, caring women who would drop out of the rat race and stay at home barefoot and pregnant, leaving men free to make all the money and have all the fun. At the start of the nineties the catwalks of London were full of size eight Earth Mothers carrying adorable babies who could not possibly have come out of their emaciated bodies and wearing white to symbolize their purity. They came straight out of a Laurens van der Post book, and proved very well that the opposite of power-dressing can only be powerless-dressing.

The most venal and meretricious eighties people took to the nineties camouflage in a big way – think of Edina in *Absolutely Fabulous*, forever chanting to Buddha for a quick fix or a freebie – but Diana had always been caring and sharing and so felt no need of a disguise. In her snappy suits, a woman who meant business, Diana was very clearly a woman now, not a girl, and as her marriage (and how much it always seemed her marriage, not theirs!) deteriorated as the eighties became the nineties, she fought back as a woman sure of her worth would.

The hysterical self-mutilation and Ophelia-like staircase-flingings were long gone; no more throwing up or falling down for this victim turned vamp turned champ. She fought back like a woman, with stealth and stubbornness and sarcasm. She became a scenery-eater of the coolest kind; this is the part of the Joan Crawford film when the heroine finally realizes that her man done her wrong and her fresh ingenue face turns to a hard-smiled, glittery-eyed mask for a moment before she snaps back to normal, or at least what passes for it. From now on it's just me and the kids. And I'll do anything for those kids. D'you hear me? Anything!

Diana of the Sorrows probed by the lenses of a thousand proxy bridegrooms

At the Taj Mahal she sat immaculately alone for the photo opportunity of the decade; Diana of the Sorrows probed by the lenses of a thousand proxy bridegrooms, like a mass Moonie wedding with only one possible bride; the Impossible Princess. And when they tracked down their stand-in and saw him walk triumphant from the field in order to kiss his lovely bride, they caught the frozen moment of his humiliation as she turned her head and made him look – his plain ageing face definitely not enough to take him beyond the velvet rope – every inch the loony stalker who had got just a little too close to the Princess of Wales and been royally snubbed for his presumption.

At a London music college, the assembled media could hardly conceal their audible yawns as the Prince was prevailed upon to toy tentatively with a cello. But as he played the first note, the Princess in full Valkyrie mode strode across the stage, sat down at a grand piano, threw open the lid and crashed into the opening bars of *Rachmaninoff's Piano Concerto No. 2.* Every camera swung round to her, leaving the Prince playing for his own amusement. And for hers.

In a moment of high camp worthy of Joan Crawford and Joan Collins poured into one Adrian gown, she even cleared a room at one of those Highgrove Set parties where her husband and his mistress generally clung to each other like drowning men running a three-legged race and told Mrs Parker-Bowles to 'leave my husband alone'. By this stage, of course, with Prince Charles quietly moved from Kensington Palace to Highgrove and communicating with his wife by memo only, with the intertwined 'C' and 'D' on their notepaper coldly uncoupled and set alone, the medium, not the message, was important. Just as women mainly dress for other women, not men, they often display territorial behaviour over men they no longer care for simply to show the other woman that she has not picked a pushover.

Sometimes her set pieces went wrong. When her father Earl Spencer died from pneumonia in a London hospital in March 1992 Diana was away on a skiing holiday in the unfortunately titled resort of Lech in Austria. With typical upper-class tenderness, none of his four children was with him when he died. They had fallen out over his plans to sell off a selection of family heirlooms, including a number of Old Masters, in order to 'tart up', as Diana put it, the run-down estate. Raine Spencer, ever her mother's daughter, had discovered that nothing succeeds like hard work, and had taken to doing stints in the estate's gift shop. Diana went particularly ballistic when she learned that her father had sold merchandising rights to a Japanese clothing company entitling them to make copies of her wedding dress.

The death of a parent often acts as a catalyst in relationships as the younger generation suddenly becomes the older gener-ation and looks around with dismay to see what a mess their predecessors have made of things, as older generations are wont to do. When Diana was told of her father's death, she decided to fly home alone, creating the chance for a photo-opportunity that would make the love-in at the Taj Mahal look like a passport photo booth. When all else failed, the Queen was called upon to remind Diana over the telephone that she was a subject as well as an object. And the Royal Family extracted once more what they wanted from her; first children, now photographs of the Heir Apparent being a supportive partner in a caring, sharing marriage. When the last shutter stopped snapping, the togetherness went the way of all royal flesh and the couple went their separate ways, to their separate homes and separate lives. The *Red Shoes* had danced Diana a long way from Norfolk, but they had brought her back to a place she had always known. Loneliness.

As a scenery-eater, she excelled; as a man-eater, she never convinced

As a scenery-eater, she excelled; as a man-eater, she never convinced. Until the end, when she seemed to find happiness with someone as outsiderish and emotionally scrambled as she was, Diana's taste in men was truly diabolical. Because of this, it was easy to forgive her. When it was time for the black sheep jumpers owned by the teenage Lady Diana Spencer to hit the Oxfam shop, Anna Harvey was at hand to help her refine and create her very own style and taste in clothes. There was no one around to help her with men. Her mother remote, her stepmother loathed, the friends she had grown up with found the likes of chocolate penises the height of riotous wit – what was she supposed to do? Married as a virgin to a man both physically and emotionally repellent, and repelled by her, it would have been nothing short of a miracle if Diana had come to maturity with good taste or judgement when it came to men.

But once again, as with her shyness and her lack of academic qualifications, what first appeared to be a defect was somehow mysteriously alchemized into a plus. The single men she dallied with when she was married and the married men she tallied with when she was separated – as though she thought, having been taught early by her parents and her husband, that the triangle was the natural form of adult human romantic behaviour – had one thing in common. They were ridiculous and they made our hearts bleed for her. 'Oh, poor girl. Think how *desperate* she must be.'

Of course she took lovers; she was profoundly the product of a class whose corruption and boredom and hypocrisy had set in stone the institution of sexual incontinence within marriage a long time ago. What is surprising is just how little the lovers ever took her. Most women are belittled by public confessions of sexual misconduct – but when Diana looked up at Martin Bashir and said in response to their pre-arranged question about whether she had slept with James Hewitt 'Yes, I adored him. Yes, I was in love with him. But I was very let down', a nation fell all over again. Nothing rubbed off on her but the ratings; her popularity soared once more.

Of course she took lovers; what else was there to do with all that useless beauty? But unlike her husband, she had not gone into her marriage besotted with another person – unless it was the man she thought he was. She had not turned to a third person until the marriage was well and truly dead, unlike him. And unlike him, she would never get over the fact that the marriage which she had entered into 'with so much hope in my heart' had shattered so quickly. It was this very apparent willingness of the heart which confirmed her in the week of her thirtieth birthday in 1991, as the most popular member of the Royal Family of all time, despite the very public dissolution of the dream. By this time, that part of the national psyche which was Diana's knew, we just knew that she had lovers. She was only flesh and blood, after all, and that's why we loved her. And if we couldn't be there to comfort her. . .

What neither we nor her husband knew was that she had embarked on a relationship with a man she had never met alone, face-to-face, one-on-one, but which was to be the most redeeming alliance of her life so far. She did not write to him every week, as she did to James Hewitt as he fought in the Gulf War, and she did not telephone him every day as she did to James Gilbey as he saw active service in the War Of The Waleses which was now burning up the Fleet Street wires each day with increasingly sly and slanderous salvos from his camp and her camp. Instead she sat alone in her drawing room at Kensington Palace, surrounded by paintings of the ballerina she might have been and photographs of the sons she might have kept. She sat there alone as the evenings lengthened and spoke into a tape recorder as if to make a living will, answering page upon page of written questions from the man who dared, Andrew Morton, her words spilling out like Scrabble letters onto an empty board, scrambled at first but soon taking shape under the hand of an expert. As the testimony grew into a text, it was passed back to her through friends to read; on at least one occasion, she wept as she read back her own true story. The girl who had devoured the sweet nothings and happy endings of Barbara Cartland now looked upon her own fairytale and saw it for what it was; a tragedy, but one which would make her stronger if only she could find the nerve to see it through to the end.

Once upon a time, to the young girl Diana Spencer, a happy ending had meant to live happily ever after with the man of your dreams. Now, to the grown woman, it meant the chance to live honestly rather than happily, with no man rather than a man who made your whole life a lie. No one had helped her, but Diana Spencer, 'Thicky' Spencer, had finally found wisdom.

The tradition of the celebrity 'autobiography', which is in reality the work of a ghost writer, is now so established that it no longer shocks us – that this or that feted personality is in actuality such an abject fool that they cannot even place in order the events of their own lives. But the book which was published under Andrew Morton's name in the summer of 1992 was a first; a book in which the ghost writer was the actual subject and the name on the jacket the medium, the familiar who had helped her find a voice.

And to anyone who knew Diana, the voice was unmistakably hers; a still, small voice torn between speaking words of oceanic global healing and cataloguing the wrongs that had been done to her from Day One – an often moving, sometimes slightly silly cross between Angel of Mercy and Recording Angel. 'I can just hear her saying those words,' the Prince of Wales told his private secretary. 'Those are her words, exactly.'

So recognizable was the voice to her husband, in fact, that the day after the first extract was published in the *Sunday Times* of 7 June – revealing her long affair with bulimia nervosa, her nodding acquaintance with suicide and the emotional tenancy of her husband's heart by Mrs Parker-Bowles – the Prince and Princess of Wales met at Kensington Palace and decided, at last, to formally separate. The day before, on seeing the open letter to him which was currently causing a million traditional English breakfasts to go cold, the Prince had gone to the Queen at Windsor Castle and floated the idea of divorce. To a very vain man – 'Your great achievement is to love me!' – from a social stratum where troublesome wives had once been easily executed for displeasing their husbands, we can only imagine his rage and frustration.

Ever cautious, the Queen made clear her wish that they should attempt to sit it out. But ever callous, with the lack of common decency which had characterized her behaviour throughout the whole affair (and marriage), she invited Camilla Parker-Bowles and her husband into the Royal Enclosure at Windsor Great Park to watch Camilla's longtime lover play polo on the same day that the Morton serialization began. They were, of course, extensively photographed by the press.

This, then, was our beloved monarch, whom we were raised to idolize and revere and send happy and glorious; unable to offer a well-meaning, true-hearted girl a helping hand as she undertook a mass of public duties completely alien to her upbringing, yet endlessly tolerant of the woman whose presence had, more than anything, made her eldest son's all-important marriage unviable from the start. Whatever the changing fortunes of the House of Windsor, no matter how disapproving the public mood towards the 'hangers-on' and shallow, callow youngsters, the inherent decency of the Queen remained unchallenged. In her inviting of Mrs Parker-Bowles into the Royal Enclosure, in this very public insult to her daughter-in-law, we could see in one terrible glance that the Queen was as cruel and hypocritical as the rest of her wretched class. Diana had once likened the Windsors to the Mafia; 'The only difference is that these muggers wear crowns,' Kitty Kelley has her telling a cousin, and like Prince Charles before us we can recognize the voice – mocking, mulish and at tether's end. Now they rallied, regardless of right and wrong.

Prince Philip surveyed the wreck of the son he had raised – faithless and vain and incapable of genuine empathy even with his own wife – and wrote him a letter praising his 'saint-like fortitude', refusing to either look at or speak to Diana during the Royal Ascot of the following week. That treacherous carriage-chasing crone, Lady Fermoy, happily reprised her betrayal of her daughter in order to keep in with the Windsors by visiting Highgrove a few days later and extending to Prince

Diana

Charles the sympathy she had been so conspicuously unable to offer her daughter and granddaughter when their husbands had misused them to the point of abuse.

Questioned by her sister Jane's husband, Sir Robert Fellowes, the Queen's private secretary, Diana denied any participation in the book. That Diana was a liar there is no doubt – 'Diana Spencer, if you tell one more lie like that, I am going to make you walk home.' And her capacity for deceit – 'Diana Spencer is the most scheming little girl I have ever met' – was one of the personality traits which made her more, not less, attractive and admirable to women, if not men. Without her scheming ways, she would have been too sweet; it was the dash of lemon in the honey which made her a classic female heroine. Who remembers Melanie Wilkes next to Scarlett O'Hara?

Deceit, like drunkenness, is one of the litmus tests which detects serious misogyny in a man. There are many men who can accept and even dignify a male drunk, but for whom an intoxicated woman is beneath contempt. A male liar and fantasist may often be admired as a cad and a chancer – indeed, in the money markets of the world, such men are the self-proclaimed Masters Of The Universe and their favourite game called 'Liar's Poker'. But a female schemer instantly inspires name-calling, especially Biblical name-calling; Delilah, Lilith or even Eve herself with that boring old Golden Delicious. Such is man's fear, apparently, of female fleetness of thought compared to their own lumbering brainwaves that only the most bovine, straight-down-the-line of women can be trusted not to make a fool of him. An honest woman is an obedient woman.

A lying woman is a rebel. And for an idealized woman to be uncovered as a liar can shock beyond all else. In his moving *New Yorker* eulogy to the Princess he knew and, literally, loved, Clive James is every inch the disillusioned lover as he remembers the way she sipped her tea and the way she told her whoppers:

> No, she wasn't always the straight goods. She often pretended. . . Then, when the news came out, you found that she had been watching you lead yourself up the garden path. It could hurt. No, I don't think she was being malicious. . .There was just a lot of stuff she couldn't share. At least once, however, she lied to me outright.

Oh, the shameless hussy! What she lied to poor bedazzled Clive outright about was, of course, the Morton book: 'I really had nothing to do with it. But after my friends talked to him I had to stand by them.' She lied to save herself and she lied to save face and she lied to save time but sometimes, it must be said, she lied for the hell of it because deceit, when all is said and done, is one of the greatest taste thrills on earth, and she was a lonely and wholesome young woman honed and poised to enjoy a life she was frightened of enjoying through the usual conduits of drink, food, drugs or unbridled sensuality. She spent so much time working out to make herself worthy of us, who would begrudge her a few thrilling fibs? Besides, she had been taught by the masters, the Family Windsor, that deceit was an essential part in the armour of the ruling class.

Who had ever bothered to tell her the truth? As a nineteen-year-old virgin, who had ever bothered to tell her that the man she worshipped was in love with someone else, and would never love her? It was a bit much to expect someone who had been tempered in the furnace of perfidy to be straight as a die. And anyway, her lies, like everything about her, added greatly to the gaiety of the nation.

It was a tricky time for Andrew Morton but he, and he alone it seemed, was a big boy and could take it; ironically, only he now seemed able to live by the once-royal code 'Never explain, never complain'. For his opponents, foot-in-mouth disease was the order of the day; as with Diana's assurance that she had had nothing to do with the book, the pompous and the piffling who saw themselves as the great and the good fell over themselves to condemn Morton – and make terrible fools of themselves. Conservative MPs, Lord St John of Fawsley and basically every man who got a quasi-orgasmic thrill from tugging his forelock but often confused it with his foreskin, all queued up to shoot the messenger. The delight of seeing their pop-guns eventually backfire and cover their faces with egg was more than worth the price of the ticket.

They were not to know that the editor of the *Sunday Times* had refused to publish the extracts until the two major sources, Diana's then-closest friends, Carolyn Bartholomew and James

Gilbey, signed affidavits swearing that what they had said was true. But when a few days later they saw the Princess of Wales embracing Carolyn Bartholomew across the front pages of the press and learned that the cameras had been waiting after an anonymous female caller had tipped off the Press Association that such an event would take place, the light must have dawned in even their throne-sniffing psyches. It was the Judas kiss in reverse and it was the bravest thing Diana had ever done. Now it was war.

But still the Queen sought to make it a phoney war as she seized the chance to build up her stockade. Though not vain like her son, she had been smug, believing too much that the Divine Right Of Kings (from where her power came) could survive in the sexy, mediagenic age of the Right Of The Divine (Diana's). She had seen her subjects, throughout the coming storm, surge, swerve and stand millions deep behind Diana, the rank outsider. She had seen the crowds waving their home-made, heart-felt placards only a few days after the first excerpt from the Morton book – DIANA WE LOVE YOU – GOD BLESS THE PRINCESS OF WALES – and they must have looked to her as terrible as an army with banners. The legal separation that Diana requested was denied her and the Queen, proving once again that given any two options she could invariably pick the wrong one with dazzling consistency, sent them away with the promise that she would think about it again in six months.

It was useless; they didn't even look married anymore. This was not a marriage in trouble, but rather a marriage that was over in all but name. And without a man to protect her, Diana was to receive the standard treatment that the media, especially the tabloid press, dishes out to women found wanting in some way. Especially women wanting to be free. On her first official engagement after the Morton excerpt, Diana visited a hospice on Merseyside where the kindness of a stranger made her cry. As her tears flowed and the shutters snapped, you could almost hear the photographers licking their lips, and it seemed as though what had started out as a fairytale romance was now mutating into a new genre of sadistic pornography. No longer under the protection of a man, she had declared her desire for independence with the Morton book, and would from now on be treated like any other uppity woman who refused to know her place. To the media's eternal shame, the tears which brought out the protective instinct in the people brought out the beast in the gentlemen of the press.

the tears which brought out the protective instinct in the people brought out the beast in the gentlemen of the Press

Low paparazzi and High Tory joined forces now to bring down Diana; some with an agenda which toadied to her husband, others simply for sport. Within weeks of the Morton book's publication, the *Sun* printed a transcript of a tape it had had for more than two years, in which a shadowy amateur radio enthusiast had allegedly picked up on a conversation between the Princess and James Gilbey. It was a sad but predictable portrait of a bored, alienated married woman half-enjoying the flattery and attentions of a single man who came across as less red-hot adulterous lover than agony aunt, albeit one that was blown copious kisses. Although James Gilbey's identity was in doubt at first, the woman's voice was without doubt that of the Diana we knew, loved and felt very sorry for.

The chase was on as the press realized that Diana's bad language would sell even more copies than her good works. Previously fiercely partisan and sensitive to the public's love for her, they now became yet another of the hounds which pursued her as editor after editor went on-message to the Prince's camp with their claims that she was hysterical, obsessional, megalomaniac – in short, mad.

Pots and kettles, not to mention geese, ganders and sauces may come to mind here. But the two cases are hardly the same. The Princess was alone, cornered, with no other outside source but the press to turn to. The Prince, on the other hand, was surrounded by the most powerful family in the land, whose support for him was growing day by day. The Princess getting into a car with Richard Kay was one thing; the Prince getting

Diana

into bed with Jonathan Dimbleby was another. Yet that autumn Prince Charles announced that Dimbleby was to write the book which would attempt to make a nonsense of Diana's true story.

Their brief bright engagement and marriage had taken place in the summer of 1981; in the fall of 1992, the fall of the Waleses was played out against a suitably muted and melancholy backdrop. With the ranks of the Establishment preparing to do final battle against her, Diana consulted with her lawyers and the sad, familiar opening manoeuvres of two sides about to set asunder what God had put together started up. Following her singular instinct, the Queen dispatched them to South Korea for a 'Togetherness Tour', as Prince Charles' private secretary briefed a barely straightfaced press.

Anyone who really believes that divorce in Britain has been made too easy and is nearly always the wrong step, should take a look at the photographs of the Prince and Princess of Wales on that last joint jaunt of 1992. In their faces we see the almost existential dismay of love on the rocks; his face racked with what could either be spiritual turmoil or a bad case of heartburn, her face devoid of all its glorious animation, her eyes drowning pools of despair. They are as bereft of joy as the little couple on their epic wedding cake all those years ago, and with about as much chemistry. The body language cannot even summon the strength to spit insults, which might later be hyped up into a best-part-of-

breaking-up-is-when-we're-making-up 'volatile' relationship
alibi. No, the body language simply sighs; 'Enough. Please,
enough'.

The
sing

le girl

All alone in a great big world

Chapter **10**

Diana

Winter brought, as everyone knew it must, the formal announcement of the legal separation of the Prince and Princess of Wales. All across the realm on the afternoon of 9 December, from the ghost town pit villages of the north to the deserted seaside towns of the south, a dismayed and cynical people raised eyebrows, smirked and sighed as Prime Minister John Major made his announcement, sounding about as happy with his lot as a Speak-Your-Weight machine having to cope with the full bulk of the King of Tonga:

> It is announced from Buckingham Palace that, with regret, the Prince and Princess of Wales have decided to separate. Their Royal Highnesses have no plans to divorce and their constitutional positions are unaffected.

The PM then turned back to the real stuff of life. It was like turning off the television after the latest episode of *Brookside*. We no longer hoped for a happy ending; we would have been happy with the truth. But for some reason, unlike people in other countries, we were not to be trusted with it. The Palace had been lying like dogs for at least half a dozen years, we knew that much, and now they would lie some more, telling us that the decision had been reached 'amicably' and that the Queen and her husband 'understood and sympathized'.

There had always been an element of pity in our reaction to the Queen – stuck inside a goldfish bowl, can't answer back, wouldn't like her job! – but as the Wales saga rolled on, that

Leprosy, AIDS and the Red Cross dominated Diana's charity
work in her final years

Trying to ignore the press and the paparazzi

The now-famous *Panorama*
interview with Martin Bashir

On holiday

Diana in her last year

Announcing her withdrawal
from public life

Diana, single, happy and in love

The Queen views the thousands of tributes left after the death of the Princess

pity became tinged with, at best, loving derision. Just how stupid did she think we were? Why was this Ruritanian idea of a happy little kingdom on which the sun never set forced to go on, when it was making us such a laughing stock in the eyes of the real world? It was now beyond doubt that the Queen had made a lousy job of bringing up her own brood; wasn't it slightly presumptuous of her to insist on playing mother to the rest of us, letting us know just this much about the situation and no more?

When would the Palace stop lying to us? In the past, whenever an elected head of state was mooted by some wild republican, the words 'Richard Nixon' were supposed to be enough to turn the ingrate a sorry shade of puce. But Richard Nixon, when caught out in his lying, had had to apologize to his people and go. Apologize, for lying to the people! The idea of the Queen doing this was as unlikely as it was delightful.

The final straw came when, later in his speech, the Prime Minister insisted that their separation would not prevent Princess Diana from taking the throne alongside her husband: 'There is no reason why the Princess of Wales should not be crowned Queen in due course.' We may have been behaving like good little mushrooms, kept in the dark and fed bullshit for a very long time, but no one believed that for a minute. Not while Prince Charles at Highgrove was ordering his staff to make all the belongings Diana had not removed into a bonfire – including, with typical lack of thought for the people of Britain, many of his children's never-used toys which might have given so much pleasure to some of the millions of children raised in mind-numbing poverty. At the very top, the MC of this massacre, was a beautiful carved wooden rocking horse given to Prince William by the Reagans. This image, of beauty put to the torch by jealousy, is one which sums up the sad marriage of the Waleses far better than any official portrait.

Meanwhile it was business as usual – lies all round, and make them big ones. 'Obviously, if something has gone wrong I'm very sorry for them,' said Camilla Parker-Bowles. 'But I know nothing more than the average person in the street. I only know what I see on television.' Her husband, fifty miles away in London, denied that his wife had anything to do with the marriage or rather the lack of it: 'How many times do I have to spell it out? These stories are pure fiction.'

But best of all were the excuses put forward by Lord St John of Fawsley, the former MP Norman St John Stevas. Having spent the past twenty years attempting to convince the British people that the Family Windsor were so far above them that, rather as GIs believed of the film star Loretta Young during World War Two, they did not have to use the bathroom as we did, he now came up with the absolute corker that, as they were more massively dysfunctional than the rest of us, and on such an epic scale, they might prove a good example of a dysfunctional family to a country where one out of three marriages ended in divorce! In essence, that we should pay millions of pounds a year to a family who would show us how to screw up on a grand scale, if we were having any difficulty in getting things totally wrong ourselves. With friends like this, the Family hardly needed the newspapers' polls which found that more than half the country believed that the monarchy would be finished, with no damage to the country, by the end of the twenty-first century.

A new year brought a new scandal, as the Camillagate tapes hit the street. Whatever else the country may have disliked about Prince Charles, it had generally accepted his own vision of himself as, above all, high-minded. The almost unbelievably juvenile, though genuinely affectionate smut he spoke to his mistress on the three-year-old tape brought to mind nothing so much as that other great British institution, the *Carry On* film ('I fill up your tank'; 'It's like that programme *Start The Week*; I can't get started without you'; 'I'm going to press the tit on the phone'; 'I wish you were pressing mine!') and cast further doubt on whether Diana had really been so lacking in intellectual stimulation for him as his friends had put about. Perhaps she had simply refused to or been incapable of indulging in bedtime banter more suited to Barbara Windsor and Sid James than Charles Windsor and his wife.

Whatever the rights and wrongs – or the 'ins and outs', as Charles and Camilla might have put it – of the tape, Prince Charles had been caught with his trousers down and would now have to enter the knockabout mainstream of common English life whether he liked it or not. For years he had striven to speak the little man's language, and now he found himself speaking a version that was thought rather too saloon bar for the lounge's liking. He was booed at his next official engagement and faced with opinion polls which claimed that only one in three of his future subjects thought him fit to be king. In Australia the Prime Minister's wife refused to curtsy to him. A proposed condom advert showed the Waleses kissing on the Buck House balcony on the day of their wedding with the caption: APPEARANCES CAN BE DECEPTIVE. USE A CONDOM. When the Palace objected, a spokeswoman said 'We really could not care less what the Royals think. The benefits far outweigh any offence it might cause to the Queen.' Even the natives were restless; off in the far-flung Fiji Islands, where the decency, tolerance and good nature of the people had let them tolerate all manner of royal rudeness, the government announced that it was to discontinue celebrating Prince Charles' birthday as he 'no longer represented greatness' to them.

At this point, Prince Charles might have learned a lesson from recent events and told the truth for once. Mocking though the public was, there was a sense that such smuttiness marked him out as One Of Us, at last, after all – naughty but nice, saucily skittish and therefore British, and not the gloomy Graeco-German bellyacher that he had always come across as. If he had made a clean breast, as it were, of the whole thing, and even held a press conference where he made a joke or two about such carryings-on, we might have welcomed him back into the fold if not into our hearts, that were bulging with Diana's extra luggage which she had just moved out of Highgrove. But he couldn't, in the end; he was too cold, too much a Saxe-Coburg-Gotha, too grand to nudge, wink and tap his nose at the common man. Instead his in-house magazine, the *Daily Telegraph,* whitewashed their front page in his honour: PRINCE OF WALES CHOOSES THE CELIBATE LIFE. The lying would go on, in short, and with it went any chance of redemption for him.

But even though nobody could find a tape on which Diana claimed that she would probably be reincarnated as a Tampax, as her husband did, she was soon to face public censure of her own. Up against her husband, in both meanings of the phrase, the Princess had looked wonderful: bold, modern and compassionate. But then, up against him, a two-toed sloth would have looked wonderful. Standing alone, her weaknesses and foibles stood out for all to see.

She started well. In the early summer of 1993 she forced reconciliations with her grandmother Lady Fermoy and with her stepmother Raine, to the amazement of her siblings. In May she scored high on the cerebral as well as emotional front when five hundred people spent a day at the Queen Elizabeth II Conference Centre debating the future of the House of Windsor. Here, at last, were real intellectuals interested in the monarchy – not the Sir Laurens Flowerpot Men variety, there only to provide Charlie with a knee to play Grasshopper at – and their verdict was a definite thumbs down. 'Something has died, and that something is the enchantment of the British people for the monarchy', said Professor Stephen Haseler.

It hadn't died, of course; it had merely changed horses all those years ago when a blushing kindergarten teacher fixed the public gaze in the headlights of her eyes and smiled, very slowly, for the first time. And Diana, though never seen nor heard to be backing republicanism, had been the unwitting searchlight which had been turned on the ruling house and found it wanting. It was 'that fucking family' whom the republicans now put on trial, and she was the veiled, unseen figurehead, a cross between Saucy Nancy and Britannia or perhaps a high-stepping, beautifully shod Trojan Horse. Old 'Thicky' Spencer, imagine; just what the intellectual republican movement had been waiting for.

She began to put together the life of a modern urban single working woman; if it could look soulless and narcissistic, then that was the price she had to pay for shaking off too much luxury and regimentation. The days were taken up with correspondence and meetings, most of them associated with her charities. It was a life such as she probably never imagined she would live and a life which many women suddenly found themselves living once the long party of the eighties was over; to come all that way, with so much hope in the heart, only to find oneself alone on a sofa, flicking through magazines, waiting. Except this time she wasn't saving herself for anything. She was just saving herself, and that was as much as she could hope for.

No doubt she had hoped to regain in some measure the brief, ordinary life she had lived in Earl's Court as a charring teenager; it was not to be. Too much, too young had happened to that delicate, strange psyche, never that solid to begin with, and it took all the Princess's therapists to put Diana, or at least hold Diana, together again. As in the old song, she had played the House that can't be beat, and they had taken away a lot of her life as punishment for her wanting it back. Then they had tossed her some remnants and told her to get on with it. But it was a sad life still, even if it was more hers. Her boys, for instance. She had been the best mother that this lousy, cold, dysfunctional dynasty had ever seen, and they had even found a way to ruin that. They had somehow turned the woman who was the embodiment of righteous motherhood into a Weekend Father, picking up her sons from school and taking them home to watch television while she watched them. She knew she wouldn't have them for long and it must have been hard staying cheerful for them, especially that Christmas when she spent Christmas Eve with them before returning home alone on Christmas morning. She was a lesson to all women, stand up for yourself and we will break your heart.

It was the sick who saved her, as they had done before. In India and Nepal, at hospices and orphanages, with Untouchables and lepers, refugees and amputees, she did what she was good at; she gave. The key to understanding the Princess's attitude, and the place in the hearts of the people that it won, is that she acted as other royals did only during times of war. She put herself out as the Windsors only ever dreamed of doing when there was morale to rally and cannon fodder to supply; and even then, it must be said, the idea of the Queen Mother eating Spam off a silver plate does not quite trump Diana embracing an Untouchable or TLCing a leper. Back in Britain, she frequented shelters for the homeless and refuges for battered women; talking to one woman who had killed her husband by pouring petrol on him and setting him alight as he slept, Diana embraced her and said 'You have been so brave'.

In the first six days of March 1993 alone, a survey showed that Diana had accumulated more than three and a half thousand column inches of newsprint and her estranged husband less than three hundred. It was inevitable that the Palace, while declaring itself an ancient institution far above photo-opportunities, sound-bites and public relations, would grow envious. They were, let us not forget, the Firm – Prince Philip had put his foot in it again, apparently, when he floated the Family as a disciplined, profit-making concern. Because now we saw the Firm in all its overmanned, underachieving, outdated disarray. And what did they do, as dying monoliths always do when something new and true comes along? They sent in the heavies.

And now perhaps, after a way-long roll-call of viciousness and a heavy-hitting register of malice on the part of the Palace against Diana the Good, comes the lowest blow of all; the one that makes the least sense and provokes the greatest suspicion that the interests of the United Kingdom and the Family Windsor are not actually one and the same after all, but sometimes – gasp! – even opposed. Because as Diana set her sights on making her life a useful one, and in the process taking the national profile of the British monarchy irrevocably out of the Dark Ages, the Firm stepped in and stopped her.

She wanted to be President of the British Red Cross; they stopped her. She asked the Palace to recommend her as head of UNICEF; they wouldn't. When she was asked to deliver the Richard Dimbleby Lecture on the subject of AIDS, the Palace forced the invitation to be withdrawn. The *Evening Standard* wondered sarcastically in an editorial why the Palace didn't just place the Princess under house arrest when her appearances might detract from those of her unpopular in-laws.

Deprived of the things she loved most – her sons, reaching out – she turned inwards, to her body. But this time she chose not the bulimia of the self-loathing but the exercise of the self-protecting. For months on end the only photographs of her we saw were photographs of her going to and from the gym, her dark glasses and long coats making her look like some parody of Shy Di, the teen who won a nation's heart. Except this time she wasn't running shyly, but rather running scared. Because now she was alone, and because her life was 'boring' from a photo-opportunity angle, a certain class of photographer had overstepped the invisible line in the sand of decency and was actually creating the events in order to sell pictures. Diana angry, Diana shouting and best of all, Diana crying. As the men – and they were always men – stuck their cameras in her face and laughed as she cried, it was not difficult to see this development as the final revenge of the ugly on the beautiful. To be blunt, for these men stalking Diana, it was the nearest they would ever get to having sex with a beautiful woman.

In November the venereal voyeurism which could at last be directed openly at Diana now she no longer wore the Royal

Diana

Warrant reached a vile climax when the Mirror Group's papers printed a series of photographs of her wearing a skintight turquoise leotard, her legs wide open, big vulnerable eyes staring straight at the camera. It was a classic full frontal porn shot, distinguishable only by a thin layer of spandex and a shoulder press. More strikingly than anything, they were photographs of a woman not under protection, and therefore up for grabs.

The owner of the gym, one Bryce Taylor, had taken eighty-two such photographs and received in excess of £100,000 from the Mirror Group for them. He boasted: 'What I did was sneaky, surreptitious and preplanned. But if I told you I had a legal scam that didn't hurt anyone and would make you a million pounds, wouldn't you say yes?' To such people, Diana was now not a person – it 'didn't hurt anyone', after all – but a commodity, something which produced money as conveniently as a cash dispenser outside of a bank.

The Mirror Group resigned from the Press Complaints Commission, and the editor called himself 'a ratbag', but any real contrition was conspicuous by its absence. Ratbags weren't really ashamed of themselves; they were cads, a bit of a lad, and Lad Culture (an oxymoron if ever there was one) was just kicking in big-time in Britain, with its mile-wide streaks of both cowardice and misogyny. As Bryce Taylor set about making his million by syndicating his handiwork abroad, Diana obtained an injunction and sued. Within weeks Taylor was bankrupt and was granted legal aid and the renowned liberal lawyer Geoffrey Robertson QC to defend him. Robertson's team put together a case for the defence which could only succeed by thoroughly attempting to blacken the reputation and name of the victim, as in most rape cases. Employees of Bryce Taylor came forward to testify that the Princess went out of her way to solicit attention by exercising in front of a window where the public could see her; they said she wore skintight clothing and flirted with male club members. In fact, the whole point of the case for the defence seemed to rest on the fact that Diana did not conduct herself as a married Muslim woman living in Iran might – and it was one step away from deciding that a rape victim had asked for it.

Though Diana tried to proceed with the trial, the Queen intervened and the Mirror Group paid off both Diana, who gave her money to charity, and Taylor, who did not. She had won, but things had changed. Once it had been the Palace against her; she was used to that. But now betrayal was everywhere; in the newspapers which had been her comfort, in the lovers who had been her consolation. Strange days had come indeed, when Leftist Australian Republicans could add yet more ammunition to the House of Windsor's long-game to bring down a single, solitary woman who had dared only to say NO. Her detective and her chauffeur were transferred without her consultation; she responded with her own dismissals, building up a reputation as a capricious and fickle employer. The day of Sly Di, Serial Sacker, had come.

On 3 December at a charity lunch, Diana announced her withdrawal from public life. Speaking for five minutes in that determined, out-of-depth small voice which no amount of coaching had been able to render Them rather than Us, she said:

Diana

When I started my public life twelve years ago, I understood that the media might be interested in what I did. I realized then that their attention would inevitably focus on both our private and public lives. But I was not aware of how overwhelming that attention would become; nor the extent to which it would affect both my public duties and my personal life, in a manner that has been hard to bear.

She had withdrawn from us, but could we withdraw from her? That cold turkey was never really on the menu was made clear just a few weeks after her abdication speech, when the photographers out in force to take the traditional snaps of the happy family attending Christmas Day church services swarmed to Diana, ignoring even the Queen. She was clearly going to be a hard habit to break.

We needn't have worried, of course. We had developed, it sometimes seemed, a Diana-shaped hole in our souls, and if she wasn't there to fill it first hand any old rubbish would do, so long as it bore the merest hint of her scent. The year 1994 saw two books which, in the absence of the real thing, would do. The organ grinder was taking a sabbatical, and it was time for the monkeys to have their say. Though vastly different in age, class and temperament, Charles Windsor and James Hewitt bore testament to one thing; that men were Diana's Achilles heel. If there was a weak, vain, cavalier man in a roomful of strong, silent, sexy saints, she would go for the first type – the heel. That same year saw the twenty-fifth anniversary of Prince Charles' investiture as Prince of Wales. Many unfortunate things had happened to the world since then – AIDS, punk rock, Ronald Reagan – but Wales too had suffered in its own small way, as the Graeco-German puppet prince who mysteriously held sway over their ancient and dynamic civilization had become a byword for betrayal. Slanderous and unfounded the cliché may have been, but to 'Welsh' on a deal, it seemed, was about the one thing he had learned from the sons of Cymru. Now, aided by Jonathan Dimbleby, he sought to explain and complain in great detail, first in a television documentary that took two-and-a-half hours, then in a biography which took two-and-a-half forests.

Whatever their failings as parents, it is fair to say that the Queen and Duke knew their son. And they knew that the impression he would create on the people would not be a good one. His naturally dissatisfied mien, held a beat too long, comes over, not as crusading zeal but as hanky-twisting agonizing; the more he seeks to reach out to the people, the more his protected upbringing seems to throttle him. In a country such as America or France, where visible agonizing is tolerated and even admired as the mark of a man, Prince Charles might have grown up a more popular public figure. But in grin-and-bear-it Britain, it was his good-soldier wife, forever putting her best foot forward and breaking down only in the privacy of her own palace, who had won our hearts with her plucky ways.

His parents, mistress and friends warned him against the television interview, and suggested a shorter and sweeter official biography. His flunkies, though, thought differently, and urged him to put his side of the case. It may not be advisable to kill the messenger generally, but when it comes to Prince Charles' there does seem to be a good case for putting them to the sword the minute they open their mouths. Once more, as with the press campaign against Diana, what she could get away with due to her beauty, youth and vulnerability looked like the actions of a bully when his unattractiveness, age and position were taken into account. A lovely young woman portraying herself as a victim of evil, tied to the railway tracks, may evoke pity; a balding middle-aged man who lays himself down, fastens his own bonds and entreats us to look upon him kindly will provoke embarrassment more than anything else.

During the two-and-a-half-hour Dimbleby interview, *Charles: The Private Man, The Public Role* which trailed the book, the Prince of Wales sought to portray himself as many things; philosopher, farmer, sportsman, ambassador and artist. But he stuck in the public mind as one thing above all, neither Action Man nor Care Bear; adulterer. Not accidental adulterer or opportunistic adulterer, but absolutely dedicated adulterer, putting into his three separate affairs with Camilla Parker-Bowles all the effort, consistency and devotion he seemed unable to give to anyone or anything else, from his public role to his private wife.

The book, when it followed that autumn, made illuminated script out of what had merely seemed like piqued graffiti. When not talking about his mistress – 'gentle', 'warm', 'caring'; that Diana so obviously had all of these virtues made his choice sound even more perverse, especially to those who had seen photographs of the angular, leathery Camilla baying for blood from horseback – he quite simply whined. He whined about the media ('carping', 'pontificating', 'criticizing'); he whined about being overworked by his own staff ('I thought the Queen always did it,' he says, pulling a babyish face when asked to attend the Royal Command Performance); he whined about the Queen's staff and how they stopped him from doing One's Own Thing ('They drive me bonkers'.) Most seriously, when not whining about his wife ('hysterical', 'obsessive', 'violent mood swings'), he whined about his parents; the father who had 'made' him marry the three-headed, bearded lady with the nasty case of scabies, and the mother who had been 'unwilling or unable' to offer the affection the young Charles had craved.

Surveying this squawking, talking, whining, pining excuse for a man, you had to wonder if you were in the Queen's sensible shoes, you too might have found it hard to offer your whole-hearted adoration. Forty-five years of unparalleled privilege had been put into this man, and he had emerged from it the very model of premillennial dismay, with no particular talents to offer a world he clearly saw as far beneath his peculiar attributes. From the most high-minded – the Scout Association wondered why it should pledge allegiance to the monarchy when 'we extol the virtues of honesty, integrity and the sanctity of marriage. But Prince Charles does not represent those virtues' – to the lewdest lowest – the *Sun* opened a phone vote-line and found that two-thirds of those who called did not want him as their king, not now, not ever – the nation looked upon the heir to the throne that ruled over them and prayed, no matter what their reservations about her, 'God Save the Queen. And God save us from that.'

Only Diana the ballet-lover – not Diana the Good or Shy Di – could have understood, comprehended and borne the year 1994. Like Giselle or Odette or one of the other white-gowned heroines betrayed by their lovers and forced into a *danse macabre* that could only end in death or the lunatic asylum, she saw treachery everywhere she looked. And this time, we saw it too. And saw that she knew she was right, all along. The years of being taunted as a paranoid hysteric bore triumphant fruit in the sumptuous betrayals by her husband, who said that he had never loved her, and by the man she had turned to for consolation, James Hewitt, who said that he had loved her, yet still sold his memoirs for a fistful of silver. *Princess In Love*, written with the journalist Anna Pasternak, was a work of such florid worthlessness that Barbara Cartland herself might have written it. Dame Barbara had always said that Diana was a figure straight out of one of her books, bringing her virginity triumphant to the marriage bed as a gift of love. This was the flipside, the dark side of the story; her gift of love brought triumphantly to the marketplace, the sheets held up for all to see.

A woman without a Maker's Mark on her is, in the rarefied air of international celebrity, a woman whom men generally would enjoy seeing as a smashed piece of Meissen porcelain. If

there is in the masses a *Day Of The Locust*ish love-hate relationship with the high-flying adored, if a fan's wish can turn just as
easily into a stalker's kiss before dying, then famous women
embody the paradox far more than famous men. The recent
phenomenon of stalking can affect both famous men and
famous women – but in the vastly more frequent stalking of
famous women, fantasies of sex and violence feature far more
often than dreams of love and marriage, as they do when
women harass male idols.

If she is beautiful and without protection, it is generally
assumed that she has brought this state about so that she may
fornicate freely with whoever takes her fancy. In 1994, Diana
became fully sexualized as a public being, and in American
comedy shows (in a country where Mom is deified at the
expense of all other women, and where any woman who
rebels against her husband can fully expect to find herself
denounced from the floor of the Senate à la Ingrid Bergman)
Diana suddenly turned up as a slut in skits and sketches.
Jay Leno, on the *Tonight* show, even pulled a sad old joke
about Christine Keeler out of storage and dusted it down one
more time; 'Princess Diana had an accident today, but she's
recovering. Soon she'll be out of the hospital and flat on her
back again'.

In the best tradition of the witch trials, women who do
what they want are thought to be beyond the pale, asking for
it; 'it', in this case, is having her photograph taken specifically
but, generally, being thought of sexually. 'She loves it. . .she's
always wanted us to do it. That's why she always looks so

Diana

good, for us. That's why she goes to the gym every day and buys all those clothes. So we'll chase her. . .she loves it.'

Diana the Good had held sway over the world and its media for fourteen years; when the seven-year itch times two set in, it would not be easily scratched. The sad fact was that despite thirty years of feminism a woman is still easiest dealt with by reducing her to the sum of her sex organs; if her heart and her head can be left out of the equation, all the more helpful for cutting her down to size. The private Diana still carried on her good work for the numerous charities she supported, now increasingly turning up unexpectedly at shelters for the homeless with her sons, where they would play cards or chess for hours with the itinerants and inebriates. Still fearful of attracting Lady Bountiful jibes from both sides, she had by now realized that ridicule was preferable to isolation, or indeed to the sort of embarrassed, embarrassing reaction her husband would have when, after her death, he sought to follow in her footsteps and actually came face to face with an old schoolmate, now a down-and-out.

The media, though, had seen her reaching out for years; what they wanted now was to catch her putting out. And in the August of 1994 they hit pay-dirt when it was discovered that Oliver Hoare, an unfortunately named and inconveniently married art dealer, had suffered some eighteen months of nuisance phone calls, sometimes as many as three in fifteen minutes. When Scotland Yard were called in, the calls were traced to Diana's home number, her mobile phone and her sister's house.

Cartoonists fell over themselves to portray her as a big-nosed, heavy-breathing sex pest

Following Diana the Bad, here at long last was Diana the Mad, as promised by her husband and his Court. Cartoonists fell over themselves to portray her as a big-nosed, heavy-breathing sex pest, men in white coats approaching her with restraints and handcuffs. But somehow, yet again, we, her people, were not that shocked. We knew that she was delicate and complex, not Sloanily straightforward; One Of Us, not One. And this, like the dreadful men we gladly forgave her for (poor girl!), was just another example of her sad, sweet sexual immaturity. Because calling a love object's house and then hanging up when a woman answers is what teenage girls do when the hormones first kick in. Except you're meant to have grown out of it by the time the woman is his wife rather than his mother. She didn't seem to know that, which made us sad for her, but never mad at her.

She had been raised as the Terminal Feminine, after all; in a world of women clamouring to go up in rockets and down in flames, she had been raised to arrange flowers and have children. And then, on top of that, she had been chosen from all

Diana

the other pretty maids in a row to be the Princess; the ultimate Being, not Doing, job description. Her job was to look beautiful and to be married to a Prince. When she strayed from that job description, she was blocked on all sides.

Once mocked by her husband ('Diana the Martyr!') for her altruism, she would now be sniped at by his side for her narcissism, as a series of grooming bills which the Prince of Wales was liable for, hit the headlines. It took three thousand pounds a week, excluding clothes, to keep that delicate body and soul rolling along now, a figure perhaps more suitable for a much older professional beauty; everything from manicures and pedicures to tinting of the hair and flushing of the colon, from acupuncture and aromatherapy and astrologers to hypnotherapy and holistic massage. 'New Age' – meaning well-marketed old mumbo-jumbo – had become the buzz-phrase of the nineties; it gave the illusion of one being 'caring' without actually having to do anything for anyone else, and by its insistence on 'thinking globally' it supplied a vital patina of politics to the rich and famous who didn't want to actually think about real political change for fear that they might come off worse in the deal. That it appealed so much to superannuated Sloanes such as the then Duchess of York was hardly surprising; with its endless crystals, essential oils and astrology charts, it enabled the breed to carry on buying jewellery, having lots of bubble baths and reading their horoscopes as usual but with a funky, ethnic, street cred twist. Right before our eyes, Diana had gone from being a teenage char whose idea of happiness was a night in with a box of Bendick's

Bittermints and Backward Benny from *Crossroads*, to the sort of 'New Age Girl' of whom Dead Eye Dick sang: 'She has a crystal necklace/She spends a lot of cash/Though her vibes are rather reckless/Heading for a crash.' We had loved her for being so straightforward and now she had gone all hippy-dippy on us.

Without doubt her interest in things New Age was the most irritating and least appealing strand to Diana. But even in the face of such provocation as irrigated colons and spirit guides (don't ask: her beloved paternal grandmother, Cynthia Spencer) we must remember what she had been through. She had lived practically no life chronologically, but she was already old; from virgin bride to mad wife in West Wing, all but signed, sealed and committed. She had tried so hard to work, to do rather than be, and she had been thwarted. Her children, whom she had lived for, would need her less and less. It was, in the end, little wonder that like millions of disappointed women before her, old and young, rich and poor, she took refuge in the idea that there was some other world better than this. From the schoolgirl reading her horoscope in *Jackie* to the widow attempting to contact her dear departed Mr with the aid of a crafty clairvoyant, women have always been prey to fortune tellers and evil eyes; it comes with the territory of 'Is that all there is?'

On the other hand, while Diana might have been talking to her astrologer five times a day, she still wasn't talking to her window box. There were, by this stage, many things Prince Charles could have hurled at his estranged wife if only he had

Diana

been sure that they would not return boomerang-like to him;
adultery was one of them and New Age flakiness another. In
Cartland romances, the young naïf must be taught everything
by her older, worldly husband. And Diana had certainly
learned her lesson well. She was by now an adulterous spiritu-
alist with a nice line in wasting public money. With her scram-
blers and shredders and her spirit guides, this was *Diary Of A
Mad Housewife* writ large for the leisured classes. It was as low
as this born lady ever sank. It couldn't go on.

Love comes quickly and leaves slowly. The start of a marriage
is gloriously clear cut; one 'I do', one kiss, one cold knife slic-
ing through the cake and you're off. But what happens when
hate slices through the couple on the cake? Open marriage,
staying together for the sake of the children, counselling,
estrangement, separation, *decree nisi, decree absolute* – when
love breaks down, we are left with an Aladdin's cave of
tarnished weapons with which to finish it off.

Stuck in an end game, Diana waited. If she asked for
a divorce she would be free – as free as she would ever
be, anyway – but she would also be doing what the Firm
most wanted. Having performed her breeding duties, she
would walk away and leave them to regroup triumphantly:
'Never had the right stuff, that Spencer girl. A bolter, like
her mother. Legged it when the going got tough.' If she stayed,
she kept her children's world as normal as it would ever
be, and she kept her status. On the issue of what to do next,
the old-fashioned girl, still a little scared of a life she did not

know, and the modern woman, eager to strike out and see, were still in conflict. In the end she did the only thing she knew how to do, she who had received short change from her nearest and dearest; she relied on the kindness of strangers. It was three years since she had hidden behind Andrew Morton and shown him the ways of the *wayang*, the Indonesian shadow puppet play. This time she would state her case face-to-face.

If the Queen had turned up with Susan the corgi on *One Man And His Dog* or if Prince Edward had gone looking for love on *Blind Date*, the initial shock of hearing that the Princess of Wales would give an hour-long interview to *Panorama* – home of the latest Ulster ceasefire or the ceaseless Arab-Israeli stalemate – could not have been bettered. But on further analysis, it made perfect sense.

Because this thing didn't seem personal any more; it felt political. Incredibly, with the destruction of the Labour Party as anything more than a vote-winning machine by Kinnock and Blair, Diana was increasingly seen as the main champion of the poor, the dispossessed and the oppressed against the uncaring Establishment of Royal Family and Conservative government. That a grown Sloane with no O Levels came to occupy this position – to an extent where, after her death, the Labour Prime Minister would attempt to hitch his wagon to her shooting star, as though she were some late Labour hero – is one of many reasons why New Labour should hang their cynical old heads in shame.

Diana

Once upon a time it had seemed such a great big world; love had opened it up for her, but now it had narrowed down to this. The silent Sunday, the staff sent away, the quiet smiling man and the stark, staring camera. The isolated elements meant nothing; the end result was the *Panorama* interview broadcast on the night of 20 November, 1995. The woman we saw there, all in black, had come to bury the bride we had cheered that summer's day all those years ago. She had never looked worse, and we had never loved her more. Fifteen years is bound to change any face, and we are all mugged by gravity in the end, but it was clear to the most obdurate royalist that a decade and a half of mistreatment by the Windsors had transformed the smooth-skinned, bright-eyed girl literally beyond recognition. She looked like the thin person who allegedly is trying to get out of every fat person; tense, terse, haggard and fatigued. Now we knew why the fat person preferred to keep them in.

Dressed as if for a funeral, black lines around her eyes and black rings around the lines, she was not an English Rose anymore. She looked oddly stateless, jet-set thin, indeterminately tanned, wealthy but not at all well. When she spoke, though, nervous and hasty and still unaccustomed as she was to public speaking, she was still one of us; only human, trying her best, getting knocked down, getting up again. The camera no longer loved her but hey, we'd never forget that face.

She talked about many aspects of her life but most memorably, it was the confession of adultery with James Hewitt that really hit home. 'Yes, I adored him. Yes, I was in love with him.

But I was very let down.' The stark simplicity of the words was a world away from the fumbled, fusty alibis the Prince of Wales had come up with about not having taken up once more with Camilla – '. . .she has been a friend for a very long time and will continue to be a friend for a very long time' – until his marriage 'became irretrievably broken down, us both having tried'.

Once more, after all that time and all that New Age self-delusion, Diana's humility and humanity just shone through. She was not proud of herself, her body language seemed to say, but neither was she ashamed; unlike the Prince of Wales, unfortunately the only man in the world who is able to seem smug and self-loathing at the same time. Such a combination does not shriek TELEGENIC! to say the least. But Diana, harsh lighting, heavy kohl and all, still had that indescribable, unimpeachable IT.

Twenty-two million Britons watched her, and it is to be hoped that Prince Charles was not one of them. Because to turn the popular phrase on its head, this was not 'You and me against the world' but rather 'Me and the world against you'. Four weeks later, the Queen wrote to both the Prince and the Princess of Wales, asking them to divorce as quickly and as quietly as possible. As the lawyers laid love out one more time, rouged its cheeks and loosened its clothing in preparation for the final carve-up, Diana could honestly say that she left her marriage by the front gate of Buckingham Palace. And not the tradesman's entrance, cowed and bowed and there to do a job not quite made clear to her, but the way she came in.

The
Pow

er
of Love

Her death and beyond

Chapter **11**

Diana

She had come clean and everything would be all right.

Diana had always been beautiful, but from the word go there had been something secretive about her. Long fringe, head down, dark glasses – at first it could be swooned away as shyness, but in later years she would come to look furtive. That was partly why the idea of her as a pest phone caller was so sadly believable, against all the odds of being the most desired woman in the world.

Sometime in 1996, she began to look clean as never before. She had been Born Again, in the best possible way. Simply, she grew up. Her body caught up with her mind; flesh grew on those beautiful bones. She sold her dresses and gained purchase on her life. Diana had often seemed like Sandra Bullock in *Speed*, driving like a demon, fast and hard lest it all be destroyed. Suddenly she both slowed down and cut to the chase.

On 28 August 1996, the Princess became a single woman. Divorced by her husband at the behest of his mother, she received £17 million and lost her title. She was no longer Her Royal Highness and should now, according to the rules of the Court, curtsy to her own sons. One has to wonder; did their grandmother ever consider how those boys would feel about this new arrangement? The name of the Surrealist painting *The Bride Stripped Bare, By Her Bachelors Even*, seemed very appropriate. It was a sad old business and this final act of spite set the full stop on it, apparently. But Diana was a past master at turning a double negative into a triple positive by now. If 'Everything Must Go' was the new tune, she would move to it fit to beat the band.

For years, long before her separation, she had been dismayed by the way her patronage of so many charities had made her life a whirl of charity balls and ladies' luncheons when what she really wanted was to learn. It was impossible to spread your compassion so thinly and still make a difference; all she had been doing was maintaining a sparkling status quo. Unlike the other women of her class who had come before, Diana had no interest in being the name at the top of the charity notepaper; rather, she was holding out to be a footnote in history – somebody who would not leave the world the way she found it.

This was cold comfort to the hundred or so charities she wrote Dear Johns to, keeping only five which reflected the no-frills, too-little-time tenor of her new modern life. The dreamer in her kept hold of the English National Ballet, but as she said to a friend, 'Ballet is lovely. But there are people dying out there.' She didn't really need her dreams any longer, and certainly didn't need to lose herself at the ballet, like those sad girls in *A Chorus Line*. Because she knew, she must have known with her instincts, that her life was shining up a treat now, coming up roses.

Freud said, in a rare moment of lucidity, that all a healthy human being needs to be happy is work and love. All! For an Englishwoman of Diana's class, this combination would be only marginally less difficult to achieve than the Nobel Prizes for Physics and Literature in the same year.

Nevertheless, and against all odds, she was about to get what she deserved. In the last year of her life, she resembled both a beautiful work of art actually painting or sculpting itself – and, on a less lyrical level, an undertaker-lawyer, the 'Uncle' of the *Eastenders*, clearing up a private life that would soon be public property once more. Whatever, Diana was ready to meet her life at last, and she walked out to meet it in the hot sun, from the Last Chance Saloon, her heart high and her holsters empty. And truly, not a man to match her.

Her last stand was pure and true, and it completely confounded those persecutors in the Prince's camp who had tried to make her look a foolish follower of fashion by high-lighting the trendiness of her work for AIDS, or who had mocked her as a martyr when she 'hung around' hospitals, hospices or hostels for the homeless. In the warped world of the Prince's Party, humankind was so intrinsically corrupt and self-interested (an easy mistake for them to make, as they yomped between bloodletting in the countryside and bed-hopping in the city), that the only reason anyone would take an interest in anyone less fortunate was because they got a kick out of it. It is hard, alas, to explain to a frenzied foxhunter that when some people see suffering, they feel sympathy, rather than sexual arousal.

Flanked by the Red Cross and the BBC – the three of them together looking like a glorious version of what the Great and the Good could achieve if they were not mainly composed of the Bad and the Ugly – Diana went to Angola, but not before the usual suspects raised outraged voices. She 'didn't have all the facts'; she was 'a loose cannon'; the objections of Tory MPs stopped her from attending an all-party meeting on the outlawing of landmines. It was a disaster; objections had just about been sustainable on her AIDS work, with the disease's undertones of deviant sex and intravenous drug-taking, so far as Middle England was concerned, but the idea that there could be any justification for blowing the legs off five-year-old children made everyone except arms dealers retch. It was typical of the then Tory government to be so insensitive and arrogant that some of its ministers even believed they could make the case for landmines. Within weeks they were replaced by a government who banned the export and use of landmines, a policy then echoed by the Clinton administration. 'The impact she had was phenomenal,' said the Red Cross. Diana went to Bosnia for three days. She stayed serene, because she had learned by now that tears are not enough. W. F. Deedes who travelled with her wrote in the *Daily Telegraph*:

> Part of her gift in bringing comfort to those in anguish lay in this sensitive awareness of when silence is best. She was not a voluble sympathizer, quite the reverse. At some point during an outpouring of grief, she would stretch out a hand or both hands and touch the person on the arm or face.
>
> I found some of the tales we had to hear almost unendurable. Yet I never saw her lose this calm, which plainly had a most soothing effect. She saw dreadful wounds, heard horrifying stories while maintaining the demeanour of a professional nurse. Nor in the course of

those three days did I see her concentration flag; and this was remarkable because the distractions were intense. The cameramen and reporters who met her at every stop had an interest in her encounters with victims of mines, but, unlike the Angolan expedition, it was not their main interest.

Their main interest was, of course, in her private life; at last, as a single woman in love with a single man, she had one that could proudly take its place in the sun rather than the *Sun*. But it was, you felt, not her greatest concern; her work was that. At last, from such a sad, stunted beginning, feeling that she was good for nothing and that love was all, she had found love. And found also that she was so good at her work that love was no longer the be-all and end-all, the deciding factor in whether she was of value or not, but one of many pleasures she could enjoy at her leisure.

But even as she walked through the Valley of the Shadow of Death, the wires were buzzing with the slime that the gentlemen of the press, in lieu of her husband, made it their business to spread about her. She was single now so, ran their sick logic, she was theirs; back in their arms, like a virgin. And if her eyes should light upon another man and smile. . . why, why, why, Delilah?

It remains the heartbreaking paradox of Diana's life that whereas most heroes are raised above the common man for promising great things and then evaporate into corruption, idleness and wastefulness, Diana was raised up for embracing idleness and wastefulness – in the shape of the House of Windsor – and then evolved into her heroism. But the press and paparazzi felt cheated by goodness triumphant over tawdriness; to those in the gutter, someone looking at the stars will seem like a stuck-up trouble-maker.

And that is how Diana, in her fully evolved finale, seemed to them. A part of them wanted to believe that she was the insecure girl she had once been, interested only in clothes and posing and having her photograph taken. But they knew now, with the heavy hearts of thwarted lovers, that this wasn't true. No matter how good she looked in chinos and a crisp white shirt, no matter that she had never been more beautiful, with blue skies in her eyes and the future in her smile, she was beyond that now. She didn't need us to love her anymore; she was beautiful for her lover, and she got the appreciation she needed from him. We were her public, there purely for understanding and caring about the things she showed us, the things that had to be changed. Loved at last, she had transcended mass adoration.

She had once needed the media, to carry love to and from her and the masses. But now the media needed her; she was their living and their lives. The man who had freed her from her need for the approval of strangers would not be welcomed. And so adulterous newspapermen, with a daily bottle of Scotch and/or recreational drug habit, with illegitimate and/or neglected children and deserted wives, singled her lover out as a drug-taking, partying playboy. But her choice of Dodi Fayed said so much more about Englishmen than it said about her. She was not an innocent girl who believed him to be something he wasn't; she had gone that route before. No, she had simply had it with England, had it with cold men who looked permanently agonized themselves while happily inflicting torment on those nearest to them, and had it with respectability. She had married into the most reputedly respectable family on earth – and found it a maelstrom of secrets and lies. A bit of upfront, vulgar hedonism must have looked like heaven after that. A resplendent, shameless Johnny Foreigner's moll, Diana did what so many sheltered young Englishwomen do who find only heartbreak where home is; she frolicked on yachts in the Med, on and off throughout the summer of 1997. The difference was that, when not frolicking, she was trying to change the world.

And then, as the summer drew to a close, Diana did something she had always yearned to do, something which spoke to her of being a modern, adult, free woman – something which most people of advanced sensibility would consider rather clichéd and banal, but something which showed just how modest her private desires were, how everyday. She set out to spend the weekend in Paris with the man she loved.

In the early hours of 31 August I awoke with a jolt and sat bolt upright. At my side the radio told me that Dodi Fayed had been killed in Paris while travelling in a car with the Princess of Wales.

I got up and went downstairs and turned on the BBC; a totem to a time when princesses weren't hunted down tunnels next to running water – for some reason so much more awful, so much more animal than crashing in an overground street. But then she wouldn't have wanted to have lived at a time when her class was safe and smug and no one would ever have heard of her and she couldn't have changed anything.

Place de l'Alma. La Pitié-Salpêtrière Hospital. There is something horrible about dying in a country not your own, like a soldier or an exile. But then she wouldn't have wanted a world in which she couldn't feel the sun on her face or the wind in her hair. A world in which she couldn't escape from the country ruled by the family who treated her the way they treated her.

Mercedes 22OSL. Drunken chauffeur. Guest of Mr al-Fayed. That would never have happened if she'd had one of those detectives she trusted so much with her. If she'd had an English driver. But they were gone – dead, transferred, taken away in some way. And she couldn't have stood a life sacrificed to security.

I knew she was dead the moment I heard that she was badly injured. She could be either radiantly alive or she could not. But she would not lie damaged in bed, because that was the pact she had made with the sick and the dying. Her radiant health was theirs, briefly, as she sat on their beds and embraced them and they looked into her sad, sad eyes and suddenly thought 'Whatever hurts us, hurts her more.' That was her secret; that there was no pity in her sympathy. She showed herself to them, and they pitied her. And that gave them strength.

Diana

There was no pity in her because she was love. Not love in a Barbara Cartland sense or love in an Emily Brontë sense or even love in the pompous, po-faced sense that the Pope and his representatives on earth speak of it. But in the crucible of this nervous, unacademic, pretty, upper-class young Englishwoman, something strange happened and base metal became gold. 'I can say that I saw God in her when she went about what she called her work,' wrote her close friend Rosa Monckton, no meek acolyte of Diana but a passionate Christian. 'And the vast majority of this work, principally visiting the sick and the dying, was done spontaneously and in secret.'

What if she was here to show us a third way? Between pleasure-seeking and piety, between self-obsession and self-denial; a life which is lived to its fullest, with the fact that we are human animals and want to have fun seamlessly blending into the fact that what diminishes others, be it homelessness, illness or war, diminishes all of us? She came up, glorious, at a time when ideology was supposedly over, and Communism, which said that we are all in this together, had been routed by the forces of Capitalism, which said that, however governments try to cosy it up, it is every man for himself.

But Diana's creed was altruism, which is candy-coloured Communism: 'unselfishness as a principle of action'. She was the philosopher-statesman needed by a century worn out and bled dry by clever men with no instinct. Above all, she was a volunteer. She was beautiful, rich and non-intellectual; if anyone could have told the world to go to hell in its own way and spent her life caring only for herself, she could have. Yet she looked at the world with the eyes of the curious, bright child who doesn't quite understand why so many people are suffering, and she wanted to know why. There were no answers good enough – there never are – and so she did something amazing. She went out and tried to make things right.

I am the cynic of the world. The cynic's cynic. A class warrior whose personal flame for the Unknown Soldier never fades. But in this aristocratic young woman, two years and two days younger than me, I saw something that I could not sneer away. Something which, if she had been a man, or been old, or been plain, might have had the world not just swooning but had it silent, staring, speechless. *And did those feet…and was the Holy Lamb of God…and did the countenance Divine…*'Snap out of it!' I told myself: 'It was just a dream.' But as I sat for two long hours waiting to be told what I already knew at 4.41 am, that 'Diana, Princess of Wales, has died, according to British sources, the Press Association learnt this morning', I knew that something had gone before it was fully known for what it was. But perhaps that's the way they always do it.

I couldn't cry. She, in her sweetness, had done so much of that – and then stopped, realizing that tears were not enough. I went upstairs and found the one letter she had sent me; there was her Diana signature, in her Diana handwriting, just like in Andrew Morton's book.

I had written to her just after the *Panorama* interview, after talking on the telephone to my friend Dominic Lawson, Rosa Monckton's husband: 'Oh, I like her SO much!'

Diana

'Write to her, then! You're being REALLY SILLY. She'd love to hear from you!'

'Oh, it's a PEST – '

a wondering, wandering girl coming home for the last time to her people, at RAF Northolt, like the good soldier she was

He rightly hung up on me, and I wrote a modest short note congratulating her on her testimony; that seems a far better word than 'performance', as used by the Prince's Party. Within a week the thick, creamy envelope, stamped with a 'D', arrived, and it was a brief note but with HER, and all her HERNESS, written all over it. She used the word 'perspicacious' to describe me, which I had to look up, so I was well impressed, but her PS made my heart feel like a blancmange that had died and gone to Heaven: 'So glad you FINALLY did!'

I sat on the stairs, and I started to cry.

When it comes to twentieth-century iconography, we really have been fed a load of old rope. One blurry man jumping on the back of the car of another blurry man who might or might not be John Kennedy. A space suit, allegedly with a man inside it, floating on the end of a cord over a cratered surface, allegedly the moon. But now, at last, this sad, shimmering century had an image that was worthy of it; a wondering, wandering girl coming home for the last time to her people, at RAF Northolt, like the good soldier she was.

Epil●gue

UNFINISHED SYMPATHY

Lest we forget –

A pretty, chubby teenager in West London, running along, tripping up, trying to escape –

A woman of poise and sophistication stepping lightly, smiling, crying, forever walking in radiant slo-mo through our memories, forever reaching out –

A dignified matriarch, already with an air of the dowager about her, being stripped of her status by her sons' grand-mother, by our gracious Queen, her stripes torn off and her name formally removed from the prayers said each day for the House of Windsor, happy and glorious, by the Church of England. England, their England –

Her in all her Herness, not her HRHness. Her; just her. Every falter, every fainting spell, every mistake, every misdemeanour, every step of the way. Love is not love that changes when it alteration finds; our love, letting her grow up –

Just her, and no one ever to replace her –

Her, loser and still champ –

And then the darkness, and nothing else.

We won't forget her.
Goodnight, sweet princess.

BIBLIOGRAPHY

Arnold, Harry. *Charles and Diana* New English Library 1981
Bradford, Sarah. *Elizabeth* Heinemann 1996
Brown, Craig. *The Book of Royal Lists* Routledge 1982
Burnet, Alastair. *In Person, The Prince and Princess of Wales*
    Michael O'Mara/ITN 1985
Cathcart, Helen. *Charles, Man of Destiny* W H Allen 1988
Courtney, Nicholas. *Sisters In Law: A Palace Revolution* Weidenfeld 1988
Fincher, Jayne. *Travels With a Princess* Weidenfeld 1990
Graham, Tim. *Diana, HRH the Princess of Wales* Michael O'Mara 1988
Grose, Rosalyn. *The Sun-sation* Angus & Robertson 1989
Holden, Anthony. *Charles, Prince of Wales* Weidenfeld 1979
Holden, Anthony. *Charles* Weidenfeld 1988
Junor, Penny. *Diana, Princess of Wales* Sidgwick & Jackson 1982
Junor, Penny. *Charles* Sidgwick & Jackson 1987
Junor, Penny. *Charles and Diana, Portrait of a Marriage* Headline 1991
James, Clive. *No New Yorker* 1997
Kay, Richard. *Daily Mail*
Kelley, Kitty. *The Royals* Warner Books 1997
Kortesis, Vasso. *The Duchess of York Uncensored* Blake 1996
Lacey, Robert. *Majesty* Hutchinson 1977
Lane, Peter. *Prince Charles; A Study in Development* Robert Hale 1988
Moore, Sally. *The Definitive Diana* Coronet 1991
Morton, Andrew. *Diana's Diary* Michael O'Mara 1990
Morton, Andrew. *Diana – Her True Story* Michael O'Mara 1992
Morton, Andrew. *Diana – Her True Story In Her Own Words*
    Michael O'Mara 1997
Pearson, John. *The Ultimate Family: The Making of the Royal House of Windsor*
    Michael Joseph 1986
Pimlott, Ben. *The Queen* HarperCollins 1996
Sakol, Jeannie and Latham, Caroline. *The Royals* W H Allen 1988
Wade, Judy. *Charles and Diana, Inside a Royal Marriage*
    Angus & Robertson 1987
York, Peter. *The Official Sloane Ranger Diary* Ebury Press 1984

INDEX

14–16; divorce 20–22; 2nd marriage 34; at Diana's wedding 7–8, 67–8; death 167

Spencer, 9th Earl, Charles Edward 5, 15, 144, 145

Spencer, Cynthia, Countess 205

Spencer, Lady Diana *see* Diana, Princess of Wales

Spencer, Georgiana, (later Duchess of Devonshire) 10–11

Spencer (later Fellowes), Lady Jane 15, 33, 44

Spencer, Sir John 9

Spencer, Raine, Countess 34, 40, 167, 189

Spencer, Lady Sarah 10, 15, 33, 36, 38, 44

Spencer, 2nd Baron, William 9

Spencer, Victoria, Countess 145

St John of Fawsley, Lord 176, 186

Stark, Koo 100

Stewart, Rod 146

Sunday Times 43, 172, 176–7

Sun newspaper 59–60, 94, 150, 179, 199–200, 216

Taj Mahal 165, 167

Tatler, 44

Taylor, Bryce 194–5

Thatcher, Margaret 113, 147, 163

Times, The 19, 148

Travolta, John 79

Trump, Donald 136

Vanity Fair 43–4

Versace, Gianni 126

Vogue 115, 127–8, 133

Wade, Judy 151

Wales 113–15, 117, 118, 132, 197

Walker, Catherine 129

Wallace, Anna 38, 48, 84

Wellesley, Jane 38

West Heath School 33, 34–5

Westminster Abbey 5, 7

Westwood, Vivienne 149

William III, King 97, 99–100

William, Prince 13, 112, 124, 135–6, 140–41, 143, 157, 191

Willis, Bruce 123–4

Wilson, Harold 84

Windsor Castle 83